THINGS TO MAKE AND DO
VOLUME 10
NIKKI McCLURE
2008 CALENDAR

Nikki McClure

Extra Arms

Sesame Le...

buyolympia.com

Clarity Miller

Sarah Utter

Tiny Meat

Arcana Soaps

I'm Smitten

Sherwood Press

Sara O'Leary

Puckish

Emily Ryan Lerner

Sam McPheeters

Jesse Reklaw

Jill Bliss

Little Otsu

Volume 05

Craft:
transforming traditional crafts™

Special Section
PAPERCRAFT

Columns

Features

Vol. 05, Nov. 2007. CRAFT (ISSN 1932-9121) is published 4 times a year by O'Reilly Media, Inc. in the months of January, April, July, and October. O'Reilly Media is located at 1005 Gravenstein Hwy. North, Sebastopol, CA 95472, (707) 827-7000. SUBSCRIPTIONS: Send all subscription requests to CRAFT, P.O. Box 17046, North Hollywood, CA 91615-9588 or subscribe online at craftzine.com/subscribe or via phone at (866) 368-5652 (U.S. and Canada), all other countries call (818) 487-2037. Subscriptions are available for $34.95 for 1 year (4 issues) in the United States; in Canada: $39.95 USD; all other countries: $49.95 USD. Application to Mail at Periodicals Postage Rates is Pending at Sebastopol, CA, and at additional mailing offices. POSTMASTER: Send address changes to CRAFT, P.O. Box 17046, North Hollywood, CA 91615-9588. Canada Post Publications Mail Agreement Number 41129568. Canada Postmaster: Send address changes to: O'Reilly Media, PO Box 456, Niagara Falls, ON L2E 6V2.

Carla Sinclair
Welcome

>> Carla Sinclair is editor-in-chief of CRAFT magazine.
carla@craftzine.com

The Power of Paper

You can rip it, wear it, recycle it, and use it to craft just about anything imaginable.

One of my first jobs as a teenager was wrapping presents during the holidays at a place called Wrapping Unlimited. I loved learning how to perfectly measure and fold the paper, conceal the tape so that the paper looked nearly seamless, cut fancy tips on the ribbon, and make ornate, handmade bows. I felt like a sorceress, transforming ordinary items into bright, mysterious parcels that glittered with enchantment.

Of all the materials we use to craft (which is just about anything, really), paper seems the most magical to me. Paper dolls and cardboard forts were ingredients for many of my childhood make-believe worlds. My durable white paper pants and airbrushed paper hoodie in the 80s seemed surreal (paper clothes that didn't rip!). Even now, a blank piece of paper, with its limitless possibilities, inspires in me a strong eagerness to create.

A blank piece of paper inspires in me a strong eagerness to create.

Of course crafting with paper also brings us two important earthly concerns: 1) industrial paper-making is one of the world's leading causes of highly toxic air and water pollution, and 2) about 9% of paper is still made from old-growth forests, which are impossible to replace.

The good news is that we don't have to use trees to make paper. In fact, paper was originally made from bark, hemp, and cotton rags — trees didn't enter the picture until the 1800s. And there's currently a growing movement to make pollutant-reduced, tree-friendly paper not only from recycled paper, but also from other pulp sources such as hemp, bamboo, and the plant fiber kenaf. I even found some stunning paper made from very thin slices of fruit and vegetables at my favorite paper store, Hiromi (hiromipaper.com).

Another alternative to industrial tree-made paper is to make your own! And in this special Papercraft issue of CRAFT, we'll show you just how to do it, with junk mail, scraps of paper and fabric, glitter, leaves, flower petals, and other goodies usually destined for the recycling bin (*page 132*).

After making your own paper, let it spring to life with both our jumping paper toy project (*page 138*) and our pop-up greeting cards (*page 54*). Or roll it into shiny, colorful beads (*page 47*). Save your road maps to weave a basket (*page 124*). Save your lunch bags to make a paper-sack scrapbook (*page 100*), or to include in your decorative "stab binding" notebook (*page 97*).

Take a peek into the lives of origami master Robert Lang, who shows us how to get fancy with a dollar bill (*page 50*), and folk-singer-turned-paper-artist extraordinaire Phranc, who demonstrates how to make a custom gift box (*page 42*).

Whether or not you actually make a gift box, we have dozens of other non-paper projects that — if you can part with them — will make perfect gifts. Some of these include our T-shirt "T-skirt," modern heirloom quilt, Norwegian felt slippers, knitted "fish" scarf, marzipan confections, papier-mâché hat stand, and a vintage-style jewelry box. To come full circle, we'll give you ideas to creatively wrap presents in ways that are resourceful, unique, and, shall we say, quite enchanting!

Finally, starting with this issue of CRAFT, we're happy to announce that our pages are now made with 30% post-consumer recycled paper. We're proud of this big jump from the 10% post-consumer recycled paper we've been using, and hope it makes even a little difference. ✕

Craft:™ Projects

Craft:
transforming traditional crafts™

EDITOR AND PUBLISHER
Dale Dougherty
dale@oreilly.com

EDITOR-IN-CHIEF
Carla Sinclair
carla@craftzine.com

CREATIVE DIRECTOR
Daniel Carter
dcarter@oreilly.com

MANAGING EDITOR
Shawn Connally
shawn@craftzine.com

DESIGNER
Katie Wilson

ASSOCIATE MANAGING EDITOR
Goli Mohammadi
goli@craftzine.com

PRODUCTION DESIGNER
Gerry Arrington

SENIOR EDITOR
Natalie Zee Drieu
nat@craftzine.com

PHOTO EDITOR
Sam Murphy
smurphy@oreilly.com

COPY CHIEF
Keith Hammond

ASSOCIATE PUBLISHER
Dan Woods
dan@oreilly.com

ONLINE MANAGER
Terrie Miller

CIRCULATION DIRECTOR
Heather Harmon

STAFF EDITOR
Arwen O'Reilly

ACCOUNT MANAGER
Katie Dougherty
katie@oreilly.com

CONTRIBUTING EDITOR
Phillip Torrone

MARKETING & EVENTS COORDINATOR
Rob Bullington

CRAFT TECHNICAL ADVISORY BOARD:
**Jill Bliss, Jenny Hart, Garth Johnson,
Leah Kramer, Alison Lewis, Matt Maranian,
Ulla-Maaria Mutanen, Kathreen Ricketson**

PUBLISHED BY O'REILLY MEDIA, INC.
**Tim O'Reilly, CEO
Laura Baldwin, COO**

Visit us online at craftzine.com
Comments may be sent to editor@craftzine.com

For advertising inquiries, contact:
Katie Dougherty, 707-827-7272, katie@oreilly.com

For sponsorship inquiries, contact:
Scott Feen, 707-827-7105, scottf@oreilly.com

For event inquiries, contact:
Sherry Huss, 707-827-7074, sherry@oreilly.com

Contributing Artists:
Melinda Beck, Scott Beale, Laurie Coughlin,
Nick Dragotta, Gabriela Hasbun, Katherine Kiviat,
Erika Larsen, Tim Lillis, Garry McLeod, Beth Perkins,
Jeffrey Rutzky, Jen Siska, Robyn Twomey,
François Vigneault

Contributing Writers:
Tina Barseghian, Susan Beal, Kent Bell, John Boak,
Joost Bonsen, Susan M. Brackney, Susie Bright,
Annie Buckley, Bonnie Burton, Cathy Callahan,
Sally L. Converse-Doucette, Laurie Coughlin,
Nick Dragotta, Marcia Friedman, Diane Gilleland,
Saul Griffith, Matt Hawkins, Christine Haynes,
Amy O'Neill Houck, Julie Jackson, Mister Jalopy,
Eileen Kirkham, Katie Kurtz, Matt Maranian,
Brookelynn Morris, Ulla-Maaria Mutanen, Jane Patrick,
Christy Petterson, Phranc, Jean Railla, Stephanie Scheetz,
Liecel Tverli Scully, Eric Smillie, Tiffany Threadgould,
Wendy Tremayne, François Vigneault, Dora Renée Wilkerson,
Megan Mansell Williams, Hillie Wurtman

Interns: Matthew Dalton (engr.), Adrienne Foreman (web),
Lindsey North (crafts)

Customer Service cs@readerservices.craftzine.com
Manage your account online, including change of address at:
craftzine.com/account
866-368-5652 toll-free in U.S. and Canada
818-487-2037, 5 a.m.–5 p.m., Pacific

NOW GREENER THAN EVER!
CRAFT is now printed on recycled paper with
30% post-consumer waste and is acid-free.
Subscriber copies of CRAFT, Volume 05,
were shipped in recyclable plastic bags.

Craft:™ Volume 05

Crafter Profiles

Inside the lives and workshops of:

Make Cool Stuff

138

ON THE COVER
These gifts are wrapped in styles created by John Boak, who uses found materials such as packing foam, leftover tissue, and ribbon scraps (learn how on page 58). The red gloves were made by Yaeko Yamashita, whose slippers are shown on page 27. The cover was photographed by Garry McLeod and styled by Ameliana Komstra/Artists Untied (who also served as our lovely hand model).

Christine Haynes and **Kent Bell** (*Party Dress*) are creative, independent, active, hard-working, fun-loving, 30-something artists. For giggles, Kent spends time surfing, skateboarding, and drinking beer on the beach with friends, while Christine rides her bike, learns to knit, and plays with their cool cats, Sally, Pinta, and Lloyd, in their vintage Venice Beach, Calif., bungalow. Christine and Kent recently unveiled their Spring 2008 collection. twospace.com

A modern renaissance woman, **Ulla-Maaria Mutanen** (*Linkages*) writes, develops, crafts, and researches. When she's not hard at work, she enjoys reading, dancing Tango Argentino, and going to flea markets. Ulla lives in the center of Helsinki, Finland, with her spouse and new baby boy. Her favorite color is black and her favorite tool is her bike. Check out thinglink.org for Ulla's social network of design.

Stephanie Scheetz (*Paper Bead Bangle* and *Bagalope*) was born and raised in Northern California. Her passion for crafting is matched only by her devotion to her four cats and her longhaired Chihuahua, Mocha. She has been a craft designer and instructor for major rubber stamp companies for 15 years. Her work has appeared in numerous craft industry and consumer magazines, in addition to catalogs, advertisements, and how-to books. You can learn more about Stephanie and her current projects on coolcrafting.com.

A diehard New Yorker, illustrator **Melinda Beck** (*Modern Crafting* and *Susie's Home Ec*) grew up in Manhattan, married a man from Queens, and lives in Brooklyn. She loves to sew clothes for her two girls, and often takes field trips with them to Mood Fabrics in the garment district. Taking time off work excites Melinda, almost as much as working on Christmas projects in 102° weather. She adores dark chocolate, and her weapon of choice is the kneaded eraser.

Matt Hawkins (*Jumping Paper Frog*) is a constant doodler. When he's not cutting, folding, or gluing, he can be found making indie comics, playing the banjo in a bluegrass band, or watching old cartoons. Matt lives in Kansas City, Mo., with his wife, Alicia, their two kiddos, Lily and Henry, and their furry friend Maggie. He's currently putting together a book of 25 paper toy designers from around the world. His niece Meadow recently summed up the biggest problem with paper toys: "This toy does not stay together good if you try and sleep with it."

Garry McLeod's (*Wrap Art* and cover photography) love of photography was born in the drained concrete pools of California backyards, capturing his skateboarding friends with his father's camera. He turned the family's bathroom into a darkroom, and when graduation came, he headed off to photography school in Seattle. In 1995 he moved to New York. Garry has recently returned to his Cali roots, moving back with his wife (also his high school sweetheart), Terri, two children, Lucretia and Gannon, and cat, Milo. Presently, Garry divides his time between New York and San Francisco.

Megan Mansell Williams (*Rock Paper Scissors*) is a former marine biologist who writes about science and culture from her home in San Francisco. An assistant editor for the UC Berkeley College of Engineering alumni magazine, *Forefront*, her freelance work appears in *Discover*, *Inkling*, MAKE, CRAFT, and *Via*, among other publications.

Susie Bright
Susie's Home Ec

» Susie Bright is an amateur dressmaker and a professional writer.
She blogs at susiebright.com.

Lies, Damn Lies, and Pant-Making Statistics

The best solution to the dilemma of ill-fitting pants is a skirt. If you've ever beheld a man in a kilt — and sighed over how handsome he looks — you've seen the evidence that men, as well as women, look better in something that doesn't stuff their caboose into a sausage casing, or into a bifurcated tent held up with a belt.

But some of you aren't satisfied. You've read a personal ad titled, "Stunner In Jeans," and you can't get that peachy image out of your mind. OK, I'll give you three no-nonsense strategies:

1. Cheat — and learn valuable lessons while you're at it.

Order a custom pair of jeans and *participate* in the fitting. If you visit makeyourownjeans.com (a steal at $45), they'll ask you for several crucial measurements: preferred waistline, full hip measurement, thigh, outer seam, inseam, front rise, back rise, and leg opening. They provide priceless photos of how to measure accurately — a sewing class in itself.

If you can make nonjudgmental measurements, you'll get a pair of pants that make you look like a movie star. You'll grok the essence of tailoring: that people look attractive in clothes that fit — and fit is based on accuracy, not wishful thinking.

2. Have a pajama party.

Make a pair of drawstring pants, in any kind of fabric that isn't dead stiff. The fancy measurements are irrelevant. You'll look chic and feel comfortable, in about two hours of sewing time.

My drawstring sensations have included pairs of Virgin of Guadalupe cotton, Elvis gold lamé, and silky Vargas Girls on parade. How do you avoid looking like you've crawled out of bed? By wearing a close-fitting shorter top, or a drapey longer one. India had the right idea from the beginning.

❋ **Here are some tips:**

* Do *not* get a unisex pattern — they fail to fit either gender. The male and female crotch curves are distinct; it makes a difference.

* Cut out your accurate full-hip size. Don't even look at the waist measurement, unless your waist is bigger than your ass.

* Before you insert the elastic/drawstring, pull the pants on — you'll be swimming in them — and tie a long piece of skinny elastic exactly where you want them to sit. Mark *that* line with chalk all the way around, take them off, then cut off 2" above your line. Serge or zigzag the raw edge.

* Here's an easy way to make the tiny drawstring opening. Before you turn down the waistband, open up the center-front seam ½", just a fingertip-width below your waistline marks. Finish this seam opening as if it were a buttonhole, stitching a little square around the hole.

* Back to the waistband: Fold the fabric along the line you marked, and sew down the waist "tube" that you'll be threading your elastic/drawstring through.

* For the drawstring: You want it to be ⅔ fabric, ⅓ elastic. This will "snug" you gently, and it won't be too bunchy — just right, as Goldilocks would say. Cut out the drawstring according to the pattern (or make your own, the same length as your waist), and snip it in half.

  Sew a piece of ½" or ¾" elastic half the length of your waist, between the two drawstrings. Now you have a long snake with elastic in its middle. Thread it through the tube.

❋ **Try these beloved PJ-style patterns:**

* **The legendary Burda one-seam for women #3216** They get the crotch curve right.
craftzine.com/go/burda

* **KwikSew men's scrubs #2861** Make a combo drawstring/elastic instead of all elastic, and achieve ecstasy! craftzine.com/go/scrubs

* **The looks-sexy-on-every-gal, stretch-fabric yoga pant, KwikSew #3115** This is a wide, flat elastic waistband, which looks fine in stretch fabrics. craftzine.com/go/yogapant

* **The impeccably groovy Folkwear sarouelles #119** These are the exception to the no-unisex rule. They look wonderful on men and women. Great crotch gusset. folkwear.com/119.html

3. For advanced-intermediate sewers *only*: Betzina's jeans.

Get Sandra Betzina's Vogue #7608 women's jeans pattern, plus her book, *Fast Fit* (sandrabetzina.com). This is a project for folks with two sewing machines they can set up simultaneously, plus a serger.

I'm serious.

Tailored trouser-making is the culmination of an impressive sewing résumé. Making the typical prom gown is *far* easier than making a pair of jeans, so think of your perfect pantaloons as something you work up to, like a degree.

What is "advanced-intermediate"? It means you've made successful skirts, tops, and dresses, put in zippers, interfacing, facings, good-looking hems, pockets, set-in sleeves, and buttons — plus you can thread a machine with a double needle. You have a serger and aren't afraid to use it.

Once you're in the zone, Sandra's your guru. She'll ask, "When you sit down, do your jeans gap in the back?" — and then tell you how to fix it, once and for all. She understands whether you're

If you can make nonjudgmental measurements, you'll get a pair of pants that make you look like a movie star.

agonizing about your calf or your bellybutton, and then offers a brilliant solution. Her pant-making videos are inspiring.

These jeans, made with the skills and measurements Sandra advises, create a back view that inspires lyric. The critical step — and there is no way around this if you want satisfaction — is to make what's called a *muslin*, a pre-test of the crucial fitting area, in an inexpensive fabric.

You quickly cut out the pattern from the waist to the knees. You don't put in the fly, you don't do pockets, you're just getting the booty silhouette. Try your muslin on, and mark *everything* that has to move a pinch here, and a handful there. Transfer those corrections to the paper pattern, and you'll proceed to wear this thing out.

I was the biggest whiner you ever met about making a muslin. I wouldn't surrender my first *four years* of sewing, I was so outraged at the prospect. But I finally caved, and now I've made so many cute jeans it's dizzying: red corduroy, art deco floral, pinstripes, and my favorites, the black denim lycra that say "BITCH" in white graffiti all over. I get mobbed at the post office in that outfit — truly, a stunner in jeans! ✂

Illustration by Melinda Beck

Cathy Callahan
Old School

» Cathy Callahan is a crafter and window dresser. Raised in Southern California by a super crafty mom, Cathy's projects are based on the crafts she made as a little girl, and on her collection of vintage publications. She blogs at cathyofcalifornia.typepad.com.

Folded Magazine Cat

We tend to think of recycling as a more recent concern, but recycling also played a big part in crafts during the 60s and 70s. I have a big collection of vintage craft how-to books with titles like *Egg Carton Magic*, *Tin Can Doll Furniture*, *Cardboard Tube Fun Ideas*, and my favorite, *Aluminum Can Apparel*.

These books taught crafters that making things from what would normally be thrown away could be fun, creative, and a good way to save money.

In Girl Scouts, we learned how to fold old magazines into the shapes of characters and animals that were then glued, painted, and decorated. I made a turkey. To learn the technique, my troop leader must have read a copy of *Folded Magazine Novelties*, a delightful craft book chock-full of instructions for fun stuff like fish, clowns, brides, and reindeer.

Inspired by memories of Girl Scout crafts, I recently made a cat. Here are the instructions that I've adjusted and updated to better suit modern-day craft supplies and materials. ✕

MATERIALS:
Magazines (2) around 5"×7", roughly 200 pages
4" foam ball
Lightweight cardboard 8½"×11"
Craft glue
Craft spray paint foam-friendly kind
Felt
Pompom
Ribbon

» **1.** Remove covers and thick pages (subscription cards, etc.) from the magazines.

2. Fold each page of the magazine twice. First take the upper right-hand corner and fold it diagonally so the top edge meets the inner edge of the page. Next, fold the lower right corner up to meet the inner edge at the same spot as the upper corner. The magazine will fan out and stand up on its own.

3. Glue the flat backs of both magazines together.

4. Cut ears, paws, and tail from cardboard (go to craftzine.com/05/oldschool for pattern).

5. Glue on the head (foam ball), ears, paws, and tail.

6. Paint and dry.

7. Cut felt whiskers, eyes, and mouth, and glue them to the face. Then glue on a pompom nose and tie the ribbon around its neck.

They may not have realized it, but my Girl Scout leader and the writers of those craft publications (who were primarily women) were very forward-thinking in terms of reuse. I think we can all learn a thing or two from the crafty ladies of the 60s and 70s.

Photograph by Cathy Callahan

Jean Railla
Modern Crafting

>> Jean Railla is the founder of getcrafty.com and the author of *Get Crafty: Hip Home Ec* (Broadway Books). Obsessed with the craft of cooking, she blogs about food, family, and community at mealbymeal.blogspot.com.

Crafting Is for Lovers

I have a confession to make: I hate scrapbooking. Sure, scrapbooks *seem* innocent. They are, after all, just a collection of photos, journaling, mementos, and craft materials "artistically" arranged in a bound book. Fine.

But what I don't understand is why you need a whole industry to support it. Why do you need stores, kits, TV shows, books, and online depots? Why do you need to purchase a kit full of baby-pink marbled papers and fake wood borders to use in your scrapbook? Isn't the whole idea of scrapbooking to use "scraps" from your life? Isn't buying a scrapbooking kit, by its very nature, cheating? Isn't it all just rampant consumerism?

It's impossible to be a crafter and be a self-righteous boob for too long.

Evidently, I must be the only woman left in America who is not taken with the craft. According to *Simple Scrapbooks Magazine*, scrapbooking is a $2.5 billion industry, and there are 32 million "scrappers" in the United States alone. Clearly, scrapbooking is taking over.

I was thinking about this the other day as I was playing around in iPhoto, arranging recent digital

pics into a slideshow that I'd play for friends and family. I added the "Ken Burns Effect," which pans on each photo, chose Fade Through Black from a pull-down menu, allowing for nice transitions between segments, and selected a song from my iTunes collection —Johnny Cash and June Carter's "Jackson" — as my soundtrack.

The result was quite lovely and we all enjoyed it so much that I started playing with iMovie, which offered equally limited but visually appealing options for making little home movies of my family. I added a few titles, more music, some video clips, and burned the results onto a DVD.

That's when it dawned on me: I was, in my own way, scrapbooking! What are these movies but digital scrapbooks of our lives together? Sure I chose the music and the images, but all the options that made it truly compelling were pre-chosen for me by those brilliant designers at Apple.

Was I cutting and pasting my own collections of memories into real objects that could be kept on a shelf? No, I was not, because it would take too long and I wanted to put something together that would be compelling but easy. In other words, the only difference between my most recent digital craft experiences and those of scrapbookers is purely one of aesthetics! Whereas I prefer a clean, modern style and a cool soundtrack, scrapbookers like a busier, pastiche-like look. Sure, I might not like it, but maybe I need to get over myself.

What's most important is what our digital and paper scrapbooks have in common: we spent the time to make something meaningful to share with those we love.

And that's what always gets me about crafting. Up or down, right or left, kitschy on purpose or without a clue, it's impossible to be a crafter and be a self-righteous boob for too long. One day you're making fun of tea cozies, and the next day you're getting all teary-eyed because your best friend crocheted you one, and even though it's ironic, you still feel the love knowing she took the time to make it for you. ✕

Illustration by Melinda Beck

I am a judge-a-book-by-the-cover girl. As a graphic designer I am attracted to magazines that look aesthetically pleasing, and yours certainly is. I love the wide scope of articles, the covers, and the funky crafts that are so enticingly presented you can't wait to start.

I am a very strange person who loves advertising; I love the products advertised in your mag, and with the online mag, it's great to be able to click on websites. Can't wait until the next issue.

—*Danielle Grisham*

Just wanted to tell you I loved my recent issue of CRAFT. As usual I sat down and read it cover to cover. I particularly liked the article "Business Basics for Crafty Types" by Jenny Ryan.

I was wondering, and hoping, if you were planning to do an additional article or an expansion on this one that would cover copyright questions — specifically in relation to the wide availability of free patterns now, and the implication of selling products made from someone else's pattern, among other topics like how to copyright your work.

I think it'd be particularly useful to us loyal subscribers. Thanks, and keep the great issues coming!

—*Emily Hughes Armour*

Thanks for the suggestion, Emily — we must be on the same page because we have an article on just that topic slated for the next volume!

I recently received my first issue of CRAFT (Volume 04), and I am looking forward to trying out many of the projects.

I enjoyed the Project article "Custom Seat Covers." However, as mentioned in the warning on page 90, there are possible safety issues with newer cars with side (seat-mounted) airbags. The warning was appropriate, although it could be more prominent in the article.

Also, the car pictured with the completed seat covers (a Saab 9-2X or Subaru Impreza) on page 88 has side airbags, as well as a warning about the side airbags on the doorsill.

Looking forward to more issues of CRAFT!

—*Rachel Popelka-Filcoff*

Thanks for writing in, Rachel — we appreciate your feedback. It's true that the car pictured (mine) is a Subaru Impreza equipped with side airbags, but they're easily disabled, which I would strongly recommend when putting seat covers on. The North American Subaru Impreza Owners Club online has a great post describing how to do this: craftzine.com/go/subaru

I'd love to be able to keep the side bags intact, but with big, furry dogs as my primary passengers, keeping the synthetic-fabric seats clean is quite a feat!

—*Goli Mohammadi*

DARN IT!

In Jenny Ryan's "Business Basics for Crafty Types" on page 43 of Volume 04, in the first paragraph of the second column, the ghost in the machine ate up several words that should have been there. The paragraph should read:

Having a website is no good unless people find out about it, of course. "Keeping a blog or sending out some sort of update email is very important," says Heidi Kenney (mypapercrane.com), a craft-biz veteran with four years of experience under her belt. "Swapping links with other small businesses is great too."

In Matt Maranian's "Beach Ball Bench" project on page 117 of Volume 04, in the Figure F diagram, the vertical measurement on the right-hand side should read 14", not 4".

 Got something to say? Write us at editor@craftzine.com.

CHARLES FURNITURE...

Coming at ya, straight outta Dublin, Ireland! Charles Furniture is the collective brain trust of
Charles O'Toole and Patrick O'Connell, two designers who live across the pond and specialize
in funky postmodern furnishings. The Ball Boy Stool, featured above, was created with the last
tennis balls ever manufactured in Ireland. Game, set, match.

Make some Thing

SAY HELLO TO CARLO ROSSI.

This is what happens when you lock Charles and Patrick in a room with a jug of Carlo Rossi. The Jug Cluster Table features a specially designed aluminum joint system, six empty Rossi jugs and a glass top. Meant to resemble a cluster of grapes, this table has infinite possibilities. But you don't have to be a master craftsman to make something amazing. All that's required is a few empty jugs and a lot of imagination. For more jug creations and great wine info visit **www.carlorossi.com**. Now go Make Something!

Carlo Rossi

Killer Crochet

At a ball a day for the past 15 years, artist **Patricia Waller** estimates she's crocheted over 500 miles of yarn into artworks, including a bear impaled on a unicorn's horn, a roasted pig's head, a leg prosthesis, and a seven-foot suit of armor, all both playful and dead serious.

In her last year as an art student, Waller turned to yarn to escape the burdens of traditional sculpture. "I couldn't move anything I made alone," she says ruefully from her home studio in Karlsruhe, Germany. "I always had to ask someone to help me. I didn't like it."

Tired of heavy tools and heavy lifting, Waller found independence through crochet. "I take advantage of this image of 'housewife art'," she explains. "At first glance, my work appears innocent; on a closer look you discover a sort of vicious irony. When people start smiling or laughing at my work, I know that my first step to approaching them has been successful."

In her favorite series, *How to Kill Your First Love*, a dart sticks in a rubber ducky's head and scissors protrude from a bleeding doll. "Sometimes my cute, soft toys turn out to be monstrous," she says, pointing out that these pieces grapple with violence against animals and child abuse, respectively.

To begin a piece, Waller builds a form from wire mesh, cotton wool, paper, and glue. Then she conceals it in obsessively chosen yarn. On shopping trips, she often brings along her subject of the moment, a bread roll for example, to match the exact color.

Despite championing "feminine" art, Waller still can't make a pair of socks. Her disinterest in working from a pattern just might date back to her first project, a potholder she made in school when she was 9. "The piece looked so awful that my mother put it in the garbage immediately," she confesses, then adds, "I think my technique has improved since then."

—*Eric Smillie*

≫ **Patricia Waller:** patriciawaller.com

Beautiful Wasteland

Entering an exhibition of **El Anatsui**'s work at the Fowler Museum in Los Angeles, my eyes and spirit adjust to the dimmed lights and inviting quiet. Slowly, I begin to take in shimmering curtains of color that shift and glow in layers of rich texture.

The change in atmosphere feels almost magical, so it comes as no surprise to learn that in Africa, where Anatsui is from, artists are often seen as mediators of supernatural energies.

Magic or not, Anatsui's laborious creative process effects a powerful transformation; despite a luxurious appearance, these wall hangings and standing sculptures are made from trash.

When goods are shipped to Africa from other areas of the world, the means to recycle the packaging materials locally are limited, and so boxes, tins, bottles, and cans accumulate in large piles. A strong believer in making art with what's available rather than using store-bought materials, Anatsui collects the detritus and uses it for his art.

Skin of the Earth (2006), an expanse of glimmering gold punctuated with bright red and blue, is made from thousands of aluminum caps from liquor bottles, the consumption of which has drastically increased since Africa was colonized by European powers.

Each cap is carefully flattened, and the small pieces are attached in small sections using a process that recalls the tradition of weaving kente cloth. A series of silvery cones that curiously resembles a Dr. Seuss landscape, *Peak Project* (1999) is made from the circular tops of discarded milk tins.

Originally from Ghana, Anatsui came to Nigeria in 1975 and has lived and worked there ever since. As a teacher at the University of Nigeria, he has influenced a generation of young artists and is recognized as one of Africa's foremost artists. In recent years, his evocative and thought-provoking work has also gained the well-deserved attention of the contemporary art world.

— *Annie Buckley*

≫ **El Anatsui:** elanatsui.com

Photography by Steven Miller (*Floating Worlds*) and Saya Moriyasu (*Waiting Ladies*)

Pretty Functional

When does a functional object become fine art? "Being pretty *is* a function," says **Saya Moriyasu**.

Nearly 100 years after Duchamp's *Fountain*, Moriyasu (a graduate of the University of Washington's Ceramic & Metal Arts program) meditates on this age-old conundrum through small-scale clay sculptures that question the nature of utility.

Her 2005 exhibition "Lamplight Lavish Gathering" directly addressed the matter through an assortment of fanciful, functional table lamps. The exhibit also marked the first time she combined display elements with her work. Lamps were stacked on a specially commissioned table, giving the installation the appearance of a furniture showroom.

In the spacious studio that's just a couple of feet from her kitchen door, Moriyasu fires low-fire white clay at medium fire, which makes the pieces stronger while giving them a porcelain look and feel.

She also uses a lot of underglaze on unfired clay, allowing her to approach the work in a painterly manner. "The way the glaze soaks into clay is like how watercolors soak into paper," she explains.

With *Lady Portraits* — small keepsake medallions of sweet-faced women — she can be more precise with details like eyelashes, hair wisps, and necklaces.

Moriyasu was thinking about expressions of absurd optimism — namely travel fantasies and idealizations of heaven — when she began work on her *Floating World* series. A three-dimensional take on traditional Japanese woodblock *ukiyo-e* ("pictures of the floating world"), the several-tiered wooden chandeliers are arrayed with ceramic monkish figures and landscape details such as Mount Fuji-like mountains and windblown trees. Unlike the lamps, the chandeliers do not emit light. Instead, they're lit to cast shadows on the walls, generating yet more depictions of ephemeral, intangible floating worlds.

Moriyasu's first permanent public commission opens April 2008 at the new Wing Luke Asian Museum in Seattle.

—Katie Kurtz

≫**Saya Moriyasu: homepage.mac.com/saya**

Tales of the Bead

Teresa Sullivan can make seed beads laugh, cry, dance, and defy gravity. Drawing from influences as diverse as William S. Burroughs, African art, and Kustom Kar Kulture, Sullivan meticulously stitches tiny beads together to create flat tapestries and freestanding, three-dimensional forms. All of her work is made with thread and beads alone — there are no armatures anywhere, and no glue.

The Portland, Ore., artist began with beaded jewelry, but had a creative epiphany in 1994 when a friend loaned her a pair of seed-beaded portrait earrings made by Baltimore, Md., bead artist Joyce Scott.

"When I saw what graphic power these earrings had, I became really excited about this medium," says Sullivan. "I realized that beads could become a vehicle for storytelling."

Sullivan's beaded stories are often about people discovering their abilities, as in her sculptures of sci-fi-influenced heroines. But she also loves telling stories in symbol, as with her *Genericity Generosity* necklace. It depicts a tale she heard from a friend, who gave away a record album to a complete stranger on a whim and later found out that the music had changed the stranger's life.

Sullivan begins each of her pieces with the germ of a story in mind, but with no specific plan as to how she'll construct it. Instead, she lets the work evolve, drawing on a variety of seed bead stitches to make some parts of the work flexible and other parts rigid. She enjoys the process of overcoming the structural and aesthetic challenges that present themselves as a piece grows.

Sullivan is also a passionate advocate for anyone who seeks to make art. Tell her you're interested in learning to bead, and she's likely to reply, "Dive in. Don't be afraid of 'ugly' or anything else. Gain inspiration from anything you like: berry picking, trash, highfalutin art, crazy people, your grandma, your big toe."

—*Diane Gilleland*

≫ **Teresa Sullivan:** teresasullivanstudio.com

Photography by Diane Gilleland

Rag Fashion

Ida Rak was amazed by the wide availability of inexpensive clothing, shoes, and bags in California's many secondhand shops. The Israeli artist hadn't seen prices this low before and was so delighted that she purchased a handful of items on a whim.

Compelled by the idea of "making something new out of something old," Rak painted discarded paper (from the print shop where her husband worked) to use as collage material, and transformed her cast-offs into fanciful paper sculptures.

Returning to Israel in 1997, Rak didn't benefit from the camaraderie of the burgeoning California craft scene; she says wistfully that she often felt like "the only person in the world doing this kind of thing."

But her crafts found another kind of community in the worlds of fashion and design. She had made whimsical paper purses for the windows of Tiffany and Co. in San Francisco while still living in California. These inspired many more offers, including a display in the company's London store.

"Sometimes it's better to display in a Tiffany window — if you're lucky," she says, "than to display in a gallery, because not many people come to a gallery and so many people look in the windows!"

Her background in painting and fine arts, however, has also led to art exhibitions; one of her large paper collages will be in a Tel Aviv gallery in spring 2008.

Rak's works are inspired by sources as varied as Mexican textiles, a leather mannequin, and Napoleon's court. Playing with papier-mâché, found objects, and watercolors, she fashioned a pointy-toed Charleston shoe from an old sandal and a blossoming summer sandal from the remains of a closed-toe pump.

An elaborate paper dress, designed for stationery company Turnovsky, boasts pink roses and a layered skirt, all made from the store's products. Models in a New York show for Israeli swimsuit company Gottex wore her paper tiaras, purses, and giant flowers.

Working with stores and designers, Rak's paper creations grow and change with each project. "I enjoy it very much," she says. "I feel like I'm always starting something new."

—*Annie Buckley*

≫ **Ida Rak:** ida-rak.com

"A lot of guys get freaked out when they hear I'm a C120. After all, my printer speed can be pretty intimidating."

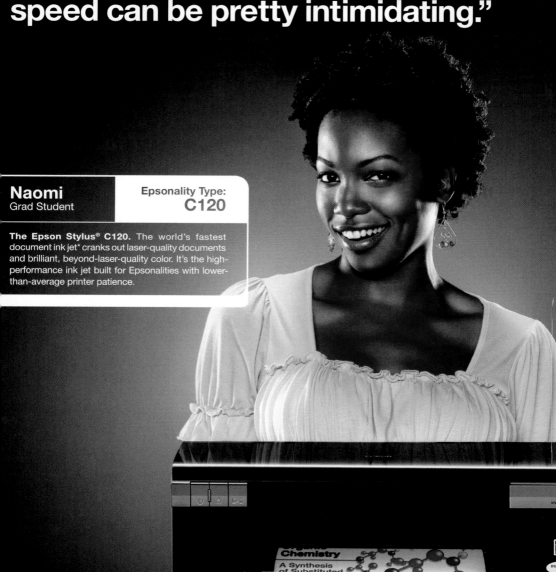

Naomi
Grad Student

Epsonality Type:
C120

The Epson Stylus® C120. The world's fastest document ink jet* cranks out laser-quality documents and brilliant, beyond-laser-quality color. It's the high-performance ink jet built for Epsonalities with lower-than-average printer patience.

Everyone's got an Epsonality. Discover yours at Epsonality.com

Marzipan Cake Decorations

Bring art motifs to your party with marzipan cake decorations. This sweetened almond paste is easy to sculpt into colorful characters or pretty designs. A plain cake can be transformed into a child's dream or a seasonal display. Create unique edible sculptures, then grab the toppings off the frosting, and eat them up.

You will need: Marzipan (sweetened almond paste, found in the baking aisle of most markets), food coloring (gel food colors work very well and come in infinite, pre-mixed colors), sculpting tools (toothpicks, knives, rollers, tweezers, anything that can be used to make an impression), wax paper

1. Color.

Set out a work surface and cover it with wax paper. Section the marzipan apart into chunks to dye. Using just 1 or perhaps 2 drops, work the food coloring into the paste. This example uses standard drops of basic colors, mixed to give a range of hues. Knead until the color is evenly spread and as dark as needed. Immediately refrigerate the colored dough on a plate until chilled through.

2. Shape.

Sculpt the cold marzipan into anything imaginable. Begin with small pieces of art. The almond paste will be sticky. To minimize this, keep fingers clean and especially dry. If it begins to stick too much to the wax paper, return it to the fridge to chill again. Creating shapes is very much like working with clay. Imagine the cake decorations as a flat cover, or as 3-dimensional designs. Either way, make the main shapes and the details separately. Pieces can be joined by roughing up the edges where segments attach, and a tiny, tiny bit of water can help them stick together.

3. Chill.

When finished making the decorations, refrigerate them once again. Then set the delicious decor atop the cake. Eat!

Brookelynn Morris has an alter ego. Her name is Princess Mountainboard, and she rides with her gang of Wildcats: the Heartthrob, the Count, the Ninja, and the Mechanic.

OUR FAVORITE TRINKETS & TREASURES

1. Curiosity Cabinet

Inspired by the 18th-century *Cabinet of Natural Curiosities*, Jessica Polka translates drawings into worsted-weight yarn, bringing the same sense of surprise that early readers must have had in seeing these creatures for the first time. She captures the astounding twists and turns that nature takes in rich, saturated colors, and tags each one like the curious specimen it is. jpolka.etsy.com

2. Jewel Thieves

This design team uses low-res screenshots of famous jewels from Google Image Search to create stunning printed and scored leather jewelry. Pieces range from Imelda Marcos' gorgeous ruby choker to a brooch digitally descended from the enormous Hope Diamond. Pixels have never looked so opulent. mikeandmaaike.com

3. Video Cross-Stitch

Joe Riedel found that the pixelated format of cross-stitch lends itself perfectly to video game images. Embroidery thread captures a tenderness and poignancy that quick-moving images lack; these bring a nostalgic smile to our faces. myspace.com/videogamecrossstitch

4. Beauty Booties

Beautiful slippers have a special place in our hearts (think *Cinderella* or *The Wizard of Oz*), and Yaeko Yamashita's are no exception, whether they're for babies or ladies. She also makes hats, clothing, and those fabulous fingerless gloves featured on page 82 with our T-skirt. lakuyaeko.com

5. Wild Things

Florence Forrest creates exquisitely beautiful toys, tapping into a magical, imaginary world (living in Australia amongst the wild things doesn't hurt) and proving that toy making truly is an art. flyingstartoys.etsy.com

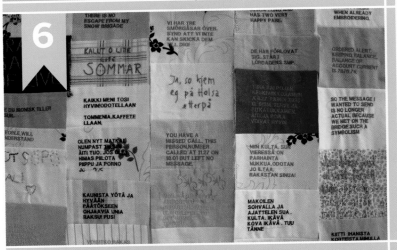

6

6. I Luv U

Ever saved a text message? Kristina Lindström and Åsa Ståhl embroider these "intimate, digital treasures," turning fleeting moments into heirlooms. They intend to create a quilt, making sweet dreams out of SMS, and revealing that brevity indeed has soul. misplay.se/ projects.htm

7

7. Bird's Eye

With pieces like *the black bird & the rose*, Diana Fayt shows that ceramics really is a marriage between drawing and sculpture. Using an elaborate hand-building process and freehand illustration, Fayt transforms clay into meditations on line, color, and shape. oneblackbird. etsy.com

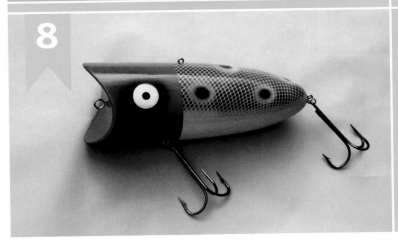

8

8. Lure Us In

There's something alluring (sorry, we can't resist a pun) about Ken Picou's oversized, retro fishing-lure sculptures. Whether you love fishing or just the eye-popping colors and shapes, take the bait. bigtimebait.com

>> TAG, YOU'RE IT!

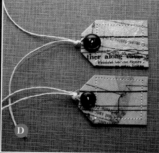

A. Kate Nydam nydampress.etsy.com

B. Gen Dalio generalgen.blogspot.com

C. Patricia Zapata alittlehut.com

D. Lisa Jordan lilfishstudios.com

E. Emma Beddard madebythem.etsy.com

F. Lisa Willis musings.willis-illustration.com

Tag Contest

We've been loving all the paper tags we see crafters making, whether it's for a hooked rug or a knit sweater, a crocheted hat or recycled jewelry. We decided to celebrate this sometimes overlooked art, and held a contest on craftzine.com.

After working on the magazine all day, it was fun to take some time to look at all kinds of tags. We saw block print tags, collaged tags, letterpress tags, handmade paper tags, modern tags, retro tags. We saw tags from all over the USA and all over the world.

The creativity involved in all of them was incredible, and we could only marvel at how lucky the recipients of your various crafty goods are to open a package decorated with one of your tags!

It was really hard to narrow it down to six winners, but we finally did. Here they are.

CRAFTER

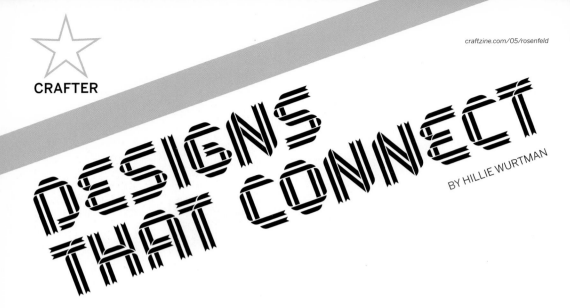

DESIGNS THAT CONNECT

BY HILLIE WURTMAN

Galya Rosenfeld's interlocking work communicates more than just clothing and jewelry.

Galya Rosenfeld's multimedia works defy the boundaries of art, fashion, design, and craft. "Usually craft and art are separated, but I never really considered that separation," Rosenfeld says. "A painting could be very precise, but at the same time could be a very flexible process, which is what design is for me. It's hard to understand where art ends and design begins."

Each of Rosenfeld's unique, handmade pieces appears to have an inner logic that is highly mathematical. Many of her works evoke the ancient, calculated craft of weaving. Her pieces are at once gentle and soft, yet playful and scientific.

In one of her latest series, Rosenfeld uses small pieces of cardboard as one of her media. All around her studio, there are square pieces of recycled cardboard paper woven together, which, as in Rosenfeld's other modular designs, form an object that can be taken apart and reassembled. In many ways it's similar to puzzle pieces, Legos, or computer pixels.

Born to Israeli parents, Rosenfeld currently resides in both the United States and Israel. In breaking the boundaries between functional design and creativity, Rosenfeld makes a statement about her places of residence. Her piece *Military Lace* is a striking necklace that looks like woven identity disc or dog tag chains. Using stainless steel ball chain material, she shows that jewelry is not only a sign of status or an embodiment of aesthetics, but can also be critical of the world around us. According

to Rosenfeld, the necklace "symbolizes so much in Israeli culture."

Rosenfeld is working on another piece of jewelry made out of simple earring hooks she soldered together as a physical representation of interconnectedness.

"It's a perfect horizon line for me," says Rosenfeld. "It's plain silver that can be made into tons of stuff. To me, its particular shape is beautiful. It inspires me."

For the 2005 "GlamMore" exhibit at the Playspace Gallery in San Francisco, Rosenfeld displayed a modular coat of animal skin patterns created from die-cut components of ultrasuede and rubber.

The modules were interwoven to create a stunning checkered textile that can form anything from bags to dresses, slippers to scarves, all depending on how the pieces are fit together. While the skins that the coat emulates can be a sign of status, they also represent the concept of survival. The design asks viewers to re-evaluate their idea of glamour.

Rosenfeld's modular coat, like many of her other designs, conveys her unique process of creation, which combines craft and design, culture and geography, technology and high concept. For Rosenfeld, the creative process is about communication. Each material speaks. Through her designs she explores the way clothing helps people communicate. ✕

Hillie Wurtman lives in Israel and studies bibliotherapy. She is a writer, yoga instructor, artist, and educator.

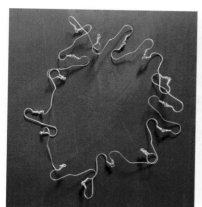

★ **CLOCKWISE FROM TOP LEFT:** Soldered earring hooks speak of interconnectedness, a necklace comments on the military, modular textiles allow wearers to re-create, Galya Rosenfeld in the studio, and a model wearing the modular coat.
galyarosenfeld.com

FROM PROZAC TO SKIN PEELS

BY JULIE JACKSON

Influenced by the surgical profession, Laura Splan crafts to create art that's fascinating and sometimes shocking.

My fascination with Laura Splan's work began with a photographic diptych entitled *Blood Scarf*. Splan describes it best:

"*Blood Scarf* depicts a scarf knit out of clear vinyl tubing. An intravenous device emerging out of the user's hand fills the scarf with blood. The implied narrative is a paradoxical one in which the device keeps the user warm with their blood while at the same time draining their blood drip by drip."

That completely blew my mind, so I wandered around Splan's website and was pleased to find a wide variety of highly imaginative work: psychiatric drugs represented in hooked-rug pillows, embroidery on what appears to be skin stretched on hoops, pillows made of meat (well, on closer inspection the blood-red and fat-white cushions are actually cotton and silk). As I dug a little deeper I discovered the duality of influences in her past, and it began to make sense that she is so wildly creative in such a precise way. I had to find out more.

Julie Jackson: First, tell us about where you grew up and how your early background in crafts evolved?

Laura Splan: I was born in Memphis, Tennessee, and raised in its surrounding suburbs. My mother comes from a family of crafters, artists, and all-around domestic divas. Oddly, my own interest in crafts didn't come until later. I think the first "craft"-related work I created was a series of large latch-hooked rug sculptures called *Prozac*, *Thorazine*, *Zoloft*. I made these for an exhibit that was part of the first Ladyfest

in Olympia, Washington, in 2000.

JJ: At the other end of the spectrum, your father and sister worked for a company that produced medical and surgical items such as implants and instruments. Do you have any visual memories of these things being a part of your childhood?

LS: My dad brought home company literature that had images of artificial hips, intraocular lenses, knee braces, and surgical drills. Sometimes he would bring the actual products home or I would see them at his office. Once he brought surgery videos home at my request, and I was able to observe a surgery with him.

JJ: I love that most of your pieces are about the thrill of the double take — the juxtaposition of the familiar and the sometimes shocking. You have a mountain of great press; have there been any upheavals, controversies, protests?

LS: The piece that has drawn the most extreme response across the spectrum of reactions is *Blood Scarf*. About a year ago, *Blood Scarf* was posted on a couple of blogs with very active readership, and some online buzz quickly spread. The comments that people have posted in response to *Blood Scarf* are fascinating — it's like being a fly on the gallery wall. I thought I had a vivid imagination, but these comments are really fantastic! Many of them are creative speculations of how the scarf works, how much blood it holds, and whether or not it would kill you.

JJ: You've said that you prefer to work with your

Photograph by Beth Perkins

Splan sits in her studio, near a negligee that was made from her own skin peel. The doily on the wall depicts a virus.

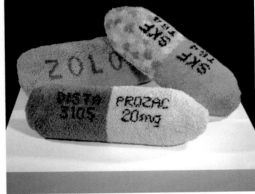

⭐ **CLOCKWISE FROM LEFT:** *Blood Scarf*, **made of vinyl tubing, may be the most controversial of Splan's work; the embroidered HIV virus is just one of the deadly viruses featured in Splan's** *Doilies* **series;** *Prozac, Thorazine, Zoloft* **is a group of latch-hook rug pillows that were mind-numbingly time-consuming to make.**

own blood in pieces like your *Wallpaper/Samples* series. What about your work that involves skin?

LS: My recent skin-related work involves sculptures constructed out of cosmetic facial peels. I apply a common drugstore peel-off mask to my entire body and peel it off in one large "hide," which is used as fabric that I embellish with embroidery. I'm currently working on a negligee, and plan to create several other objects for the series, which is called *Trousseau*. I like the idea that all of the peels have the impression of my own skin on them.

JJ: Your recent work includes intricate doilies that depict the structure of different viruses. Can you tell us about the creation process?

LS: *Doilies* is a series of free-standing, machine-embroidered doilies mounted on velvet, each design based on a different viral structure. I begin with a digital image of the virus and base a graphic design on it. The design is imported into embroidery software, where the stitches are laid out. Finally, the designs are output from a computerized embroidery

machine onto water-soluble fabric. When the fabric is dissolved, only the thread that forms the doily remains. This free-standing doily is then mounted and framed. ✂

➕ See more of Splan's extraordinary creations at laurasplan.com, or at upcoming shows Nov. 8–March 9 at the Museum of Arts & Design in New York City, and Jan. 18–March 7 at Spaces Gallery in Cleveland.

🎥 Watch Splan's doilies and other processes unfold on KQED Public Television's *Spark*: craftzine.com/go/splan

---

Julie Jackson is the author of *Subversive Cross Stitch: 33 Designs for Your Surly Side* (Chronicle Books, 2006). A total web addict, she's the force behind subversivecrossstitch.com, snarkymalarkey.com, and kittywigs.com.

Ulla-Maaria Mutanen
Linkages

Ulla-Maaria Mutanen lives in Finland and is CEO of Social Objects, Ltd., founder of Thinglink (thinglink.org), and author of the HobbyPrincess blog (hobbyprincess.com).

The Movement for Fun

Professor Kevin Henry called me one day from the Art and Design Department at Columbia College Chicago. "Do you think we're witnessing the rise of a new craft movement?" he asked me curiously. Henry explained that he had been interviewing crafters for a study he was conducting. "Almost none of the crafters I spoke with considered themselves part of a larger movement," he complained. "Most of them just craft for fun!"

People who are just having fun do not a movement make? Let's first turn around and look back at a historical precedent — the Arts and Crafts movement at the end of the 19th century. At a time when industrialization and minimum-quality mass production were booming, a group of artists and designers, activist William Morris among them, issued a call for the revival of the lost spirit of crafting in design, for a return to simplicity, sincerity, good materials, and sound workmanship. Morris' group never evolved into a social or political organization. Rather, it was a loose community of professional craftsmen who shared the same artistic ideals.

Today the story's different. First, there's a whole universe of coexisting artistic styles and aesthetic ideals. Second, today's crafters are more often hobbyists than professionals. They're also driven by various personal motives.

Take my sister-in-law Kukka, who studies history at university. She lives on a tight student budget, and perhaps because of that, crafts a lot of cool stuff. She sews her own skirts and bags, builds clever Christmas presents out of recycled materials, and paints beautiful greeting cards. She saves her pennies, and gets more delight by crafting unique creations instead of buying expensive merchandise from the store.

My journalist friend Liisa is another example. She just loves making cool things and realizing her ideas. Once, she made pillows with a wonderful cat design that grew so popular she had to make a whole bunch for her buddies. Another time she crafted necklaces and swapped them for lunches with co-workers. She also organizes crafting get-togethers. One Saturday, she had us sew outfits for going out that night. For her, crafting is about having fun with friends.

Then there is Stefan, who runs a yoga retreat. Following Mahatma Gandhi's *swadeshi* philosophy of local self-sufficiency, he rejects imported mass-produced items and always tries to find a way to support local makers and entrepreneurs. He thinks that by setting an example for others, he can help make the world a better place. For Stefan, crafting is an alternative lifestyle.

The one thing that these three have in common is the celebration of individual creativity. And that's the whole point. The emerging craft movement is not about outspoken leaders or violent controversy. Instead, it's about regular people following their passions and connecting with their friends.

> Without making a big deal about boycotting big brands or saving the environment, crafting changes the way we consume.

Still, it'd be a mistake to shrug crafters off as clueless. Beneath their innocent appearance, they are planting the seeds of change. Without making a big deal about boycotting big brands or saving the environment, crafting changes the way we consume. It exposes us to the ideals of William Morris: the preference for creativity, sincerity, good materials, and sound workmanship over wasteful mass production.

But this time the movement isn't limited to a group of professional craftsmen. Instead, it's spreading much further and broader than Morris could have imagined in his wildest dreams. ✕

Travel Crafty:
SAN FRANCISCO

BY NATALIE ZEE DRIEU

Shop your heart out for crafty goods in the City by the Bay.

The San Francisco Bay Area is famous for the Golden Gate Bridge and for sourdough bread. And while the tourists line up for a ride on the cable car trolleys, you can fill up your afternoon shopping for crafty goods and munching on yummy food with this Travel Crafty guide.

ImagiKnit
3897 18th Street
imagiknit.com

From floor to ceiling, everywhere you look you'll find yarn, yarn, and more yarn.

Allison Isaacs and the friendly staff at ImagiKnit are fantastic at helping you find the right yarn you'll need for any project. I've been coming to this store since it first opened and I always find inspiration ogling and touching all the yarns they carry.

You can also just sit in their craft book area and search for your next project through their extensive pattern binders, books, and magazines, or sit on their cozy couches and chairs and cast on your new project.

Hone your craft skills by taking any one of their classes, from knitting and crochet 101 to spinning. You'll definitely find lots of fiber love at ImagiKnit.

Food Match: Stroll across the street to Samovar Tea Lounge (samovartea.com) for a pot of green tea and their tea-infused cookie plate. Then sit back and knit or crochet in serenity.

Photography by Natalie Zee Drieu

Natalie Zee Drieu is senior editor of CRAFT and writes for the CRAFT blog at craftzine.com.

Discount Fabrics

525 4th Street

discountfabrics-sf.com

Located in San Francisco's SOMA (South of Market) district, this Discount Fabrics location (one of three in the city) has the largest fabric variety of anywhere I've been. Shop like a fashion or interior designer in this industrial warehouse setting, where large rolls of fabrics are stacked on metal racks. With wholesale prices to the public, your wallet will thank you.

You'll find everything you need in upholstery, cotton prints, Asian silks, felt, and wool. It's a great place to stock up on fabrics and supplies for special events such as a party or wedding.

The store also features all you need for sewing, including notions, ribbons, zippers, bias tape, and threads in all colors. The selection in the store changes weekly, so stop by often for sales or surprise fabric finds.

Food Match: Head on over to the District wine bar (districtsf.com), located a few blocks down on Townsend Street, for a glass of wine and a small cheese plate.

Flax

1699 Market Street

flaxart.com

Boasting 10,000 kinds of paper from around the world, art and design store Flax will reinvigorate your love of paper. Your heart may skip a beat in the paper room as you open the multitude of flat file drawers, exposing the most beautiful sheets of paper imaginable, much of it handmade.

Flax also carries an array of sketchbooks, photo albums, and stationery goods, as well as pens, pencils, and watercolor paints that will keep your creativity flowing. Shop online at flaxart.com.

Food Match: Grab lunch at Zuni Café (zunicafe.com) for one of their famous brick-oven, flatbread pizzas.

Ambatalia Fabrics

1 El Paseo, Mill Valley

ambataliafabrics.com

Take a 30-minute scenic drive outside of San Francisco to sunny Mill Valley and experience a green, sustainable fabric store, Ambatalia Fabrics.

Proprietress Molly de Vries spreads her craft love in all aspects of the shop, which feels like a cozy cottage with handmade pieces and antique décor adorning all nooks and crannies.

Ambatalia features a wide array of organic cotton, hemp, soy, and bamboo, as well as rare fabrics from France and Japan. In addition to special events and sewing classes, check out Ashley Helvey's class on how to wet-felt a stylish laptop bag.

Read more about Ambatalia and green crafting at ambataliafabrics.blogspot.com.

Food Match: For a quick pick-me-up, get a slice of dreamy carrot cake and iced coffee at the Depot Bookstore Café (depotbookstore.com).

rock PAPER *scissors*

BY MEGAN MANSELL WILLIAMS

Paper artists are turning new pages.

Sure, rock smashes scissors. And yeah, scissors cut paper. But is that so bad? After all, a handful of artists around the globe are slicing up the pulpy product in strikingly inventive ways.

Instead of sculpting with clay or pushing pigment around a canvas, they're razoring sheets into ghostly portraits, photographing books as Ansel Adams would landscapes, and constructing functional objects from bound texts.

Paper, essentially mashed-up plant material, has been a record-keeping wonder since ancient Egyptians first soaked, pressed, and dried strips of papyrus, a sedge native to the Nile Valley. And in Japan, origami — the art of folding paper — has been a pastime since the 1600s.

"Paper is inexpensive and easy to manipulate, and it can last a long time under the right conditions," says Kako Ueda, a Brooklyn-based artist from Japan who employs immense patience in her love affair with the fiber.

Ueda creates astonishing paper cutouts of "hybrid beings" using only an X-Acto knife, a technique similar to that used by the kimono-stencil makers of her homeland.

Scotland's Georgia Russell is another similarly devoted paper piercer. She painstakingly feathers the pages of found photographs, books, musical scores, maps, and money with a scalpel so that fine strips flare from acrylic frames.

"Paper is so incredibly versatile," says Australian sculptor Dan McPharlin, who renders miniature replicas of vintage synthesizers and recording equipment out of cardboard. "Working with it doesn't require expensive tools or a sophisticated studio,"

he says. "The process is relatively quick from idea to finished product."

McPharlin collects the real-life inspirations for his tiny sculptures. He simply thought it'd be fun to fashion the high-tech objects in a low-tech medium. But he's quick to point out cardboard's many sophisticated virtues. In the 1960s, for example, architect Frank Gehry pioneered the use of it for lightweight, inexpensive furniture.

One of McPharlin's biggest influences is sculptor Richard Sweeney. Based in London, Sweeney cuts, scores, and folds paper into alabaster fixtures that look like a cross between a diatom and a buckyball.

Indeed, Sweeney takes inspiration from the repetition found in nature and architecture. He has said of his work that his goal is to "create objects that are simple to construct yet complex in appearance, and are efficient in the way they are produced, both in terms of construction time and material use."

While many artists work with paper for its ease and thrift, others, like Texas photographer Cara Barer, are capturing the product's inherent beauty. By wetting the pages of phone books and computer manuals and holding them in place with curlers and clothespins, she seizes graceful sepia-toned portraits.

Abelardo Morell, a Cuban-born photography professor whose work has appeared in the Museum of Modern Art in New York, takes gorgeous black and white stills of books that seem to move with the subtle speed of glaciers. And his brain-teasing *Alice's Adventures in Wonderland* series brings

» *Abelardo Morell's "Alice's Adventures in Wonderland" series, from 1998, brings scenes from Lewis Carroll's tale to life.*

Photograph by Abelardo Morell

Clockwise from left: *Cara Barer finds phone-books and computer manuals worthy of graceful portraits. Dan McPharlin creates miniature cardboard replicas of vintage recording equipment. Richard Sweeney's* Icosahedron *blurs the lines between nature and architecture. Jim Rosenau's* Steps to Better Reading *takes a literal approach to book shelves.*

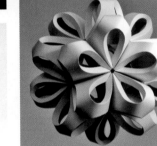

scenes like the infamous tea party to life by placing cutouts from Lewis Carroll's tale amongst a forest of life-sized books.

Some paper artists are so enthralled with their medium that they use books in their entirety as building blocks. Robert The, of bookdust.com, carves hardcovers into powerful shapes. *The Art Crisis* becomes an ominous black handgun, for example.

Jim Rosenau, of Berkeley, Calif., takes a utilitarian approach. He constructs shelves and cases out of various volumes. Rosenau, whose father and maternal grandfather were publishers, made his first bookcase from a set of 1938 encyclopedias. "Books carry so much symbolic freight," he says. "But as a material, they provide color, texture, fonts, and a pleasing form."

Furthering the leap to functionality, Takeshi Ishiguro designed a sort of coffee table pop-up for Artecnica called *Book of Lights*, from which a simple low-voltage lamp springs when the cover is cracked open. Atelier Bomdesign of the Netherlands, on the other hand, has made warm, literate lamp shades by splaying book pages around a light bulb suspended from the ceiling.

Whether today's paper artists are cutting, photographing, or building with the stuff, paper presents reams of opportunity.

➕ For more information and article sources, go to craftzine.com/05/paperroundup.

Megan Mansell Williams is a former marine biologist who writes about science and culture from her home in San Francisco. An assistant editor for the UC Berkeley College of Engineering alumni magazine, *Forefront*, her freelance work appears in *Discover, Inkling, MAKE, CRAFT,* and *Via.*

Photography by (clockwise from left): Cara Barer, Dan McPharlin, Richard Sweeney, Kim Harrington

PAPERCRAFT

A piece of paper is a hidden treasure: it looks simple, but can make almost anything. In this special section, folk singer Phranc turns unwanted cardboard into objects of desire (*page 42*), you can make magazines into beaded jewelry (*page 47*), and computational origami master Robert Lang morphs a few bucks into a priceless blossom (*page 50*). Pop-up can make any day a holiday (*page 55*), and, believe it or not, trash is easily turned into festive gift wrap (*page 58*). And making a flexagon? Now *that's* a magic trick (*page 62*).

The Cardboard Cobbler

 Folk singer Phranc surrounds herself with striking clothes and other fun stuff — all of which she's made from cardboard. **BY ANNIE BUCKLEY**

"I failed sewing three times," Phranc says, laughing. I am talking to the famed folk singer, next to a crowded worktable in her sunny art studio in Santa Monica, Calif., amid strikingly real cardboard renditions of sailor shirts, candy boxes, and a life vest.

That this quintessentially rebellious iconoclast has found the same wry sensibility in paper and paint that's a trademark of her albums — from the best known, *I Enjoy Being a Girl* (1989), to the most recent, *Milkman* (1998) — is something of a feat in itself, and doing it with spurned home-ec skills is somehow apropos. The self-proclaimed all-American Jewish lesbian folk singer punctures entrenched stereotypes with humor and humanity in her music, and her cardboard art is equally reflective, if quieter.

"I've been making stuff out of cardboard since I was a kid," Phranc says, recalling submarines and other "stuff you could crawl into." As a punk rocker in Los Angeles in the 80s, she sold her cardboard wares out of her apartment the day before rent was due. Since then, the work of The Cardboard Cobbler, Phranc's newest moniker, has come a long way. She has been included in several group exhibitions, and her first solo show opens at Cue Art Foundation in New York City in December.

Phranc has a deep respect for the everyday, innocuous little things that make our lives better, like an ice cream bar, a favorite pair of shoes, or the perfect shirt. Her art both celebrates and elevates these objects by preserving them in the simplest of media: paper and paint, cardboard and thread.

When working in paper, she first designs a pattern for her "fabric," sketched carefully in pencil. She eschews exactitude and prefers a handmade line to a ruler-straight one. Paper, Phranc explains, is unforgiving. To give paper added flexibility, she layers it with acrylic or gesso before tracing and painting the pattern. When it's time to cut the pattern and sew, she says with a smile, "you close your eyes, you say a prayer, and you hope it doesn't tear."

Memory and family are intricately connected to Phanc's cardboard work. In 1991, while she was away on tour, her brother was killed. The tragedy prompted her to take time off from music and ensconce herself in her studio, where she focused on paper creations. Her first three-dimensional pieces, realistic replicas of pumps, penny loafers, and her trademark combat boots, inspire smiles and reflection. Phranc's work reinforces a universal connection between objects, memories, and the feelings that weave them together. In her studio, a cardboard KidKraft kitchen inspired in me a visceral memory of being a kid in the 70s.

When Phranc and Lisa, her partner of ten years, started a family, it was again important to her that she not be on the road so much. So she took the beautiful black and gold Singer Featherweight sewing machine she inherited from her grandmother to a friend's house and learned to sew.

Phranc still uses her Nana's machine to make her creations. Each sewn garment includes a hand-painted label adorned with a single palm tree or ocean wave. Her label, Phranc of California, is reminiscent of growing up in California. The garments are made to be exhibited, rather than worn. But as she completes each one, Phranc slips it on just once — the perfect test-run for artwork that celebrates the joy and fragility of the here and now.

Annie Buckley is an artist and writer based in Los Angeles. She wrote the profile of artist Marnie Weber in CRAFT, Volume 04.

Photography by Robyn Twomey

PAPER PACKED: The vibe in Phranc's studio is busy and relaxed at once. Though she's continually folding, cutting, or measuring, her infectious enthusiasm and welcoming smile (not to mention homemade cupcakes) perfectly complement the brightly painted paper creations that line the walls.

How to Make a Fancy Box from Trash

By Phranc & Annie Buckley

There you are, running around the house searching for the right-sized box to package your perfect gift — maybe it's handmade or a thrift store find. Phranc, aka The Cardboard Cobbler, shows us how to turn trash into treasure for a funky, fancy, just-right gift box.

Vary the size and you have a packing box, storage box, or any kind you need. With a virtual treasure trove of great boxes waiting in the garbage, let's get going!

MATERIALS

» **CARDBOARD BOX** CEREAL BOXES, CORRUGATED BOXES, ANY CARDBOARD WILL DO

» **X-ACTO KNIFE WITH #11 BLADE**

» **PENCIL**

» **YARDSTICK**

» **SCISSORS**

» **CUTTING MAT OR SURFACE**

» **BROWN PACKING TAPE OR CLEAR TAPE**

» **METAL RULER**

» **ACETATE (OPTIONAL)** FOR WINDOW BOX

» **GOLD ELASTIC CORD (OPTIONAL)**

» **YOUR DREAM BOX** OR OTHER INSPIRATIONAL MATERIAL

Photography by Robyn Twomey (top); Annie Buckley (bottom)

START »

1. GET INSPIRED

The first step for any artist is inspiration, so start by choosing your dream box. Maybe it's a blue Tiffany box, or a red Valentine. Keep it simple! This is the box you'll use as a model, so make sure you like the shape and style.

For more advanced crafters, pick other inspirational material, maybe a pair of shoes longing for a home, or a special necklace that needs a place to rest, and make your box to fit.

2. CRUISE FOR CARDBOARD

Peruse your trash can or recycling bin — any good-lookin' piece of cardboard will do. Cereal and toy boxes are excellent choices, as are packages from medical and feminine hygiene products. Just make sure it will be a large enough box to hold your gift.

3. OPEN AND TRACE

Using your X-Acto, open up all box seams and lay the package facedown. Cut in half. These 2 pieces will be your top and bottom. Place your dream box in the center and trace. For those who like a challenge, lay your inspirational material onto the cardboard and trace an even rectangle around it. Use a ruler to draw the lines. Make each side an equal length.

4. MEASURE THE BOX SIDES

Phranc uses the width of a yardstick as her magical measuring guide for the depth of the box. For a shallow box, use 1 yardstick width. For a deeper box, increase to 2 or 3 widths to achieve the desired box depth. Placing the yardstick against your traced rectangle, use a pencil to outline the sides of the box.

5. CUT AND SCORE

Using the metal ruler and X-Acto, cut along the outside lines. Draw an X in the 4 squares at the corners of this shape. Cut along these corner lines and remove the little squares marked with the X.

Very lightly score along the inner 4 lines, folding and creasing each side toward the center to begin to form your box.

6. TAPE THE BOX CORNERS

Cut a piece of packing tape the same width as the sides of the box. Pinch together each of the 4 box corners, using small pieces of tape to secure them. For a fancier box, use clear cellophane tape, but for an everyday box, brown packing tape is best.

7. MAKE THE BOX TOP

Using the bottom of your box as a guide, turn it upside down and trace. Make sure you outline the box loosely; this will give your top a snug but comfortable fit.

Repeat Steps 3 through 6, except make the sides of the box top a little shorter to show off the bottom of the box. Your nifty gifty box is complete!

8. GET FANCY

For an added touch of glamour, cut out a rectangle from the top and fill from the inside with clear acetate. Feel free to enhance your box with paint, a gold cord, or colorful ribbon.

9. MAKE SOME STORAGE

To make large, industrial-sized boxes, follow the same basic procedure using large pieces of recycled cardboard.

In the land of The Cardboard Cobbler, your boxes and curtains, gifts and shoes, albums and books are all made to order from the same material that made your childhood forts, robots, caves, and dolls' accessories: cardboard.

Now you're a box-making expert. Adjust the dimensions and materials as you please. You'll never be without a handy box again!

➕ Phranc's cardboard creations: phrancthecardboardcobbler.blogspot.com

Paper Bead Bangle

Roll your own beads to make an awesome safety pin bracelet.
BY STEPHANIE SCHEETZ

I'm a self-proclaimed paper pack rat. Big pieces, little pieces, nothing gets thrown away. One day I sat staring at a huge stack of paper strips, all the same size. They were leftover remnants from a workshop I had prepped months earlier. "What the heck am I going to do with these?" I thought. And the challenge was made, albeit to myself. I needed to design a project that used up these last bits of paper, which others might have thrown away. What resulted was a fresh spin on a craft project familiar to many, but never seen like this.

Photography by Sam Murphy

MATERIALS

» **OLD MAGAZINES** OR OTHER LIGHTWEIGHT SCRAP PAPER SUCH AS NEWSPAPERS, GIFT WRAP, OR SCRAPBOOK PAPER

» **SAFETY PINS (30-40)** ALL THE SAME SIZE

» **ELASTIC JEWELRY CORD**

» **GLUE STICK**

» **CRAFT KNIFE**

» **CUTTING MAT**

» **METAL RULER**

» **SKEWER**

» **TAPE MEASURE**

» **SMALL PLASTIC OR GLASS BEADS (OPTIONAL)** AS GARNISH

» **CLEAR NAIL POLISH (OPTIONAL)**

START »

1. CUT PAPER INTO STRIPS

Cut the paper into 5"-long strips that are the same width as the width of the bar on the closed safety pin you're using for the project. (If you decide to add extra glass or plastic beads to the pins, take their width into consideration and adjust the width of your paper strips accordingly.) The number of strips depends on how many finished beads you'll need for your wrist size, so I recommend taking a quick measurement before you begin the project. I find it's good to start with approximately 30 to 40 strips; you can always create more if you need them. After you cut your strips, you will need to divide them in half diagonally, from corner to corner. What you'll get are 2 elongated triangles.

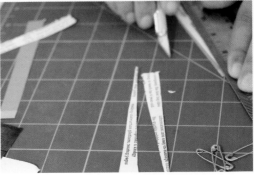

2. ROLL TRIANGULAR STRIPS AROUND SKEWER

Starting at the widest end of the triangle, roll the paper around the skewer at least once, and then apply glue to the remainder of the strip. This keeps the bead from sticking to the skewer. Continue rolling the paper around the skewer, keeping the point of the triangle in the middle.

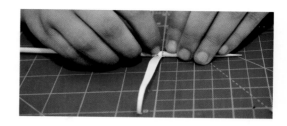

3. SECURE PAPER BEADS ON SAFETY PINS

After the bead is completed, slide it off the skewer. Place your bead on a safety pin — along with other decorative beads if desired — and close the pin to keep the bead secure. Repeat this step with the remaining rolled beads. It's helpful to lay them side by side so you know approximately how long your bracelet is getting.

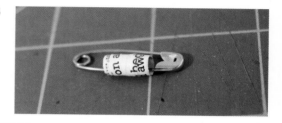

4. THREAD SAFETY PINS ONTO CORD

Cut a couple pieces of elastic jewelry cord into 10" lengths. Thread one cord through the heads of the safety pins and the other cord through the bottoms of the pins. Continue adding prepared beads until you get your desired length. Unless you want a snug fit on your wrist, I like to add 2 to 3 extra beads to make it a little looser.

After you're done threading both cords through the safety pins, tie the ends together. Make sure the knots are secure so the ends won't pull apart.

When everything looks good, trim the excess cord from the ends and put the bracelet on your wrist for others to admire and covet!

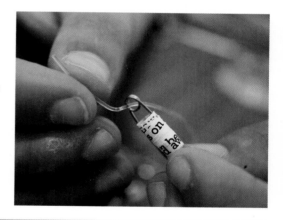

Alternative Materials and Optional Finishing

If you don't have old magazines laying around the house, you can easily substitute some other paper to make the beads. Some wonderful alternative materials might be newspapers, gift wrap, gift bags, or scrapbook paper. The key is to have the paper be lightweight and not thick like cardstock.

Personally, I like the natural finish of paper, but if you prefer having your beads look more polished, you can always apply a protective coat to the surface. This will also help prevent your beads from unraveling. You can purchase a spray or brush-on sealant for the finish, but the most frugal option is good ol' clear nail polish. Apply an even coat to the surface and allow the bead to dry on some wax paper before handling.

Stephanie Scheetz (coolcrafting.com) has been a designer and instructor in the craft industry for nearly 15 years. Some of her hobbies include thrift store shopping, eBaying, and collecting mail art, prison art, and bad art.

Folded Universe

 Origami master Robert Lang breathes new life into paper.

BY TINA BARSEGHIAN

How does a small square of paper — flat and flaccid — metamorphose into a lifelike longhorn beetle or red-tailed hawk without a single cut or a drop of glue? In the hands of master origami artist Robert Lang, anything is possible.

Take a close look at Lang's pieces and you'll notice not just the accuracy of his renderings — the detail of the tarantula's exoskeleton, the sharpness of the hermit crab's antennae — but also the objects' less tangible character traits.

"One of the things I try to do is capture the emotional impact of a subject," Lang says. "It's not

> **"Part of my motivation for folding creepy things is that I love the actual subjects."**

enough to say I've got the same number of legs as a real tarantula. I want you to feel the same thing that I feel when I look at one. A certain position of a flap one way just looks like a crumpled flap, but you position it differently and it looks like a leg. That part is much more intuitive — you have to know what works."

Art and science converge organically for Lang, whose right-brain and left-brain aptitudes perfectly complement each other. Lang worked as a physicist and engineer for many years at both Jet Propulsion Laboratory and Spectra Diode Labs, and holds dozens of patents in optics and semiconductor lasers. But it was his knowledge of origami that got him hired to develop an algorithm for airbag design and engineer an expandable space telescope.

What keeps Lang enthralled with origami, toiling away as he does in his Bay Area home creating a veritable paper wildlife refuge, is his love of animals. From the time he was a boy, Lang loved tramping in the woods and inspecting the natural world around him. "Part of my motivation for folding creepy things is that I love the actual subjects," he says.

Lang's quest for that indefinable realism has inspired him to create more than 500 original origami designs and eight books on the subject. Each time he finds a flaw in a piece, he goes back to square one and a new opus is born. "Somewhere down the road I'll see flaws," Lang says. "It's usually deep and structural, something that had forced me into a non-optimal representation that somehow got the proportion wrong or was too exaggerated. Then I'll go back and redesign it in a completely new way."

But don't mistake his drive as a meaningless quest based on vanity — it's part of his process, and what he enjoys most about the art of origami.

"I don't believe there's perfection in origami," he says. "If I wait long enough, I'll see the flaws, and I'll figure out a way I can do it better in the future."

That now includes using a laser cutter to score lines in paper for far more precise folds — and complicated shapes — than human hands alone can make.

Lang still marvels at the endless possibilities an uncut square of paper holds. "There seems to be no limit to what can be accomplished, and it's always surprising," he says. "You'd think that people would've long ago figured out all of what could be done, but in fact we're nowhere near the limit. That continues to be what's so wonderful about origami, and conversely, what keeps me going. I love creating something new or beautiful and interesting, and doing it with such limited materials."

Tina Barseghian is an Oakland-based freelance writer, contributing editor at *ReadyMade* magazine, and the author of *Get a Hobby! 101 All-Consuming Diversions for Every Lifestyle* (HarperCollins), which includes a chapter about origami.

Photography by Jen Siska

ABOVE: Master origami artist Robert Lang uses his mathematical skills, science background, and considerable artistic talents to create lifelike creatures in his Alamo, Calif., office, home to creatures like the one perched on his finger, *Simple Parrot, opus 415*, and those on his desk: *Pill Bug, opus 343, Scorpion Varileg, opus 379, Western Pond Turtle, opus 404*, and *Mount Diablo Tarantula, opus 481*. TOP RIGHT: *Dancing Crane, opus 460* MIDDLE RIGHT: *Bull Moose, opus 413* LOWER RIGHT: *Water Strider, opus 472* BELOW: *Instrumentalists*

Three Dollar Flower, opus 488

Designed by Robert J. Lang
Diagrammed by Jeffrey Rutzky

There's a distinct genre of origami that uses paper currency as the folding medium. Among other uses, moneyfolds make great tips at restaurants! But with the march of inflation, a tip of a single dollar is getting pretty chintzy. Here's a moneyfold that uses 3 dollar bills (and nothing else), which I composed as a tip at a local restaurant, Alamo Café.

START »

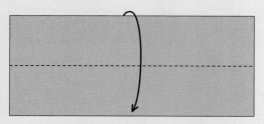

1. Green (back) side up, valley-fold in half lengthwise. Crease sharply.

2. Valley-fold in half widthwise from right to left. Crease sharply.

3. Valley-fold in half lengthwise, making a pinch mark about one-third in from the right edge.

4. Valley-fold the lower-right corner point to the pinch mark, on the angle shown. Crease sharply.

5. Mountain-fold the lower-right corner point along the angled edge made in Step 4, bisecting the upper-right corner. Crease sharply.

6. Unfold the top layers back to Step 2.

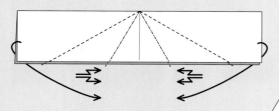

7. Pleat both layers by carefully reversing some of the existing folds made in Steps 4–5. Bring the left and right edges down to make the shape shown in Step 8. The front, back, left, and right sides should look symmetrical. Neaten all folds.

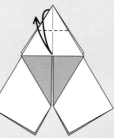

8. Valley-fold the top point down, in half, to the horizontal edge; crease very sharply. Unfold.

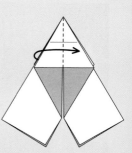

9. Book-fold the top layer from left to right.

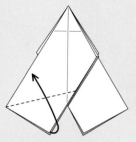

10. Valley-fold the top layer's bottom point up so that the lower sloping edge aligns with the upper sloping edge, bisecting the left corner.

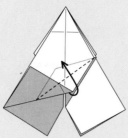

11. Valley-fold the top layer on the angle shown so the lower sloping edge becomes parallel to the left-hand sloping edge.

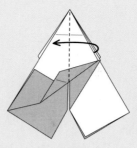

12. Book-fold the top layer from right to left.

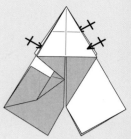

13. Repeat steps 10–11 on the right side. Turn over and repeat Steps 9–12 on the reverse side. The front, back, left, and right sides should look symmetrical. Neaten all folds.

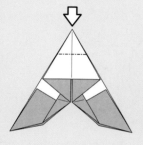

14. Open-sink the top point on the existing creases made in Step 8. Neaten all folds.

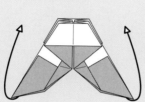

15. Unfold the sink made in Step 14.

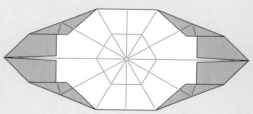

16. Flatten lightly as shown.

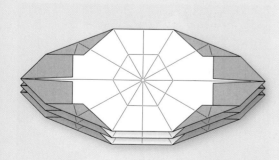

17. Repeat Steps 1–16 to make two more modules.

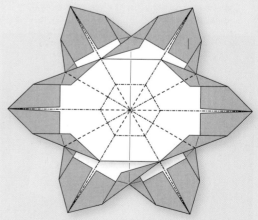

18. Align the three modules as shown, offsetting each by 120°. The folds will be aligned with one another. Refold the stack of layers, as if it were a single sheet, to the configuration of Step 15. Neaten all folds, then flatten firmly.

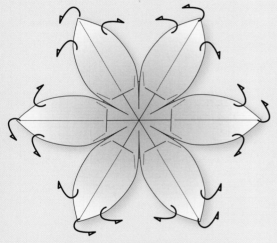

19. Open out top sink into a horizontal flat twist. Model will become 3D.

20. The result of top sink opened and flattened. Turn over.

21. Insert your index finger between the layers of each petal, separating them while pressing your thumb against the lower side where shown. Then move your thumb to the bottom of the flattened sink and pinch your finger and thumb together to set.

press thumb

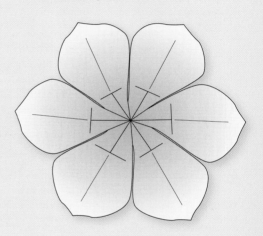

22. Curl petals outward and roll tips down. A pencil may be helpful to curl each tip against, making a uniform curve.

23. The finished Three Dollar Flower, opus 488.

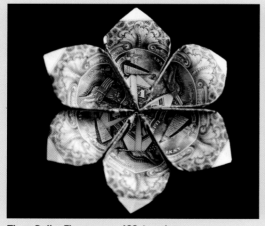

Three Dollar Flower, opus 488, top view.

Three Dollar Flower, opus 488, bottom view.

Kinetic Cards

DIY pop-up engineering.
BY BONNIE BURTON

While every great book should have characters so vividly described that they jump off the page, it's infinitely cooler to have people, creatures, and scenes that literally pop up with every page that's turned.

Pop-ups are not only exciting to read, they're even more fun to make. Whether you plan to create a greeting card complete with a birthday cake and candles, or a mini mystery book featuring a killer carrot that hides out in the crisper, you need to know the pop-up engineering basics. Here's how to get started.

MATERIALS

- » **SCISSORS**
- » **PENCIL**
- » **CONSTRUCTION PAPER**
- » **GLUE** OR GLUE STICK
- » **TAPE**
- » **MAGAZINE CUTOUTS** IMAGES AND LETTERS
- » **EXTRA DECORATIONS (OPTIONAL)** SUCH AS PIPE CLEANERS, STRING, FABRIC, GOOGLY EYES

BOX SUPPORTS

One of the most basic kinds of pop-up is the box support, which holds the object in place when the card is open. In order for the pop-up to work, you'll be making the box support on the fold of the card, so that when it opens at a 90° angle you can see the scene come to life.

1. Fold a piece of construction paper in half either vertically or horizontally.

2. Lightly draw a rectangle across the fold.

3. Cut along the lines that cross the fold, but not the end lines of the rectangle. You don't want to fully cut out the rectangle shape.

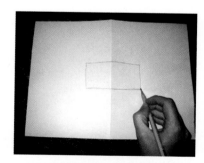

4. Push the rectangle out so that it forms a 3D box, as shown here. Tape or glue to the box the image you want to pop up when the card opens. Add to the scene inside the card with fabric scraps, magazine letters, etc.

5. Fold the card back up and make a harder crease along the fold. Glue another piece of construction paper to the front and back of the card to hide any hints of the paper engineering that's happening inside. Decorate the outside of the card with magazine letter cutouts, drawings, or whatever you want.

ACCORDION SUPPORTS

1. Fold a sturdy strip of construction paper, ideally the same color as the background of the card, back and forth like the pleats of an accordion. The shorter the strip, the better (usually).

2. Tape or glue one end of the accordion to the picture you want to support, and the other to the inside of the card.

3. This support is great for smaller pop-up items, like individual letters, googly eyes, little bird cutouts for sky scenes, cotton ball clouds, tiny kites, etc.

✛ Check out a range of pop-up styles in our online gallery at craftzine.com/05/popup.

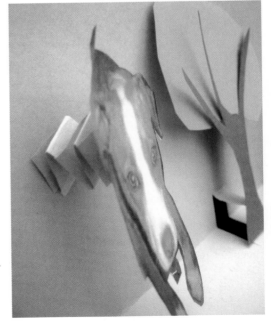

Bonnie Burton creates geektastic crafts for Lucasfilm in the Kids section of starwars.com. She's the author of *You Can Draw: Star Wars*. When she's not making pop-up cards, she can be found on her site grrl.com.

Photography by Bonnie Burton and Sam Murphy (bottom left)

Popping Up
with Matthew Reinhart

Photograph by Sam Murphy

When you crack open a book by author and artist Matthew Reinhart, you never know what crazy critter or fantastical character will jump off the page and into your imagination.

Working with Robert Sabuda (the Prince of Pop-ups), Reinhart constructed paper special effects in the *Encyclopedia Prehistorica* series and the *Young Naturalist Pop-Up Handbooks* of beetles and butterfies. He engineered *The Pop-Up Book of Phobias* and *The Pop-Up Book of Nightmares*. He then branched out on his own with his first solo book, *Animal Popposites*.

"It's a series of little pop-up flaps with opposite animals, one being drawn on the flap's cover and the other a pop-up inside," Reinhart explains. "I tried to make unconventional creatures rather than the obvious ones — for instance, a mouse was brave while the elephant was afraid."

More recently Reinhart has ventured to a galaxy far, far away with his new book, *Star Wars: A Pop-Up Guide to the Galaxy*. "I worked for a year, and during the last 4 months, 7 days a week and all day long," Reinhart says. "I was obsessed with getting everything right while still interpreting the galaxy in my unique way. *Star Wars* is one of the sole reasons I am an artist today. The collaboration of artists over the last 30 years always inspired me, and it made me see that I could make a living in the arts doing what I loved.

"My favorite pop-ups in the book are the Hoth battle on the first spread, with the stomping AT-AT; the rancor with thrashing claws (and a doomed Gamorrean in his clutches); the completely three-dimensional Millennium Falcon; and the exploded Cantina with practically all of the scum and villainy inside! The light-up lightsabers are über-cool, as well as the helmet of Vader, which ominously closes over the scarred face of Anakin Skywalker."

Among the more unusual aspects of Reinhart's *Star Wars* book are pop-ups within pop-ups, and mini plastic lightsabers that light up. "I began with just engineering the pop-up, and getting Vader's and Luke's postures just right," he says. "Once we got the saber working, I worked on creating a mechanism to turn the lightsaber on when the pop-up opens. I knew it'd be cool to see Luke and Vader dueling from across the pages."

Reinhart is now working on the follow-up series to *Encyclopedia Prehistorica*, called *Encyclopedia Mythologica*. "The first of the three volumes is all about fairies, mermaids, pixies, and magical beasts!" he says. "It's kind of weird to go from *Star Wars* vehicles, droids, and creatures, to fairies, but I like the challenge. After *Fairies and Magical Creatures*, I'll continue with *Dragons and Monsters*, and then *Gods and Heroes*. Maybe if I'm lucky, I'll get to do a *Star Wars Prequel Trilogy Pop-up Guide to the Galaxy*."

For novice paper engineers, Reinhart offers a few tips to start making pop-up books and cards.

"Try and try again — we make many, many mistakes to get to the finished pop-ups," he advises. "Look at pop-ups that you like, and try to remake them yourself. We use scissors, tape, glue, and 110-pound cardstock that you can easily find at an office supply store. Start simple, and you'll gradually get better. Pop-ups don't happen perfectly the first time, so be patient. Don't let failure get in your way; learn from a 'failed' pop.

"Sometimes we listen to the pops to hear where paper is catching or snagging. At my partner Robert Sabuda's website, robertsabuda.com, there are all kinds of make-your-own pops to print and build, complete with step-by-step instructions."

—*Bonnie Burton*

Wrap Art

Create a paper masterpiece each time you wrap a gift.

BY JOHN BOAK

As a child, one day I realized that I could wrap with any kind of paper, and I was thus liberated into wrap art. It was collage in the service of transient delight, with no greater agenda than to make random materials dance and sing briefly before the eyes and eager hands of a gift's recipient. All of these wraps rely on recycled and repurposed materials, such as shopping bags, office supplies, and crafting scraps, along with a heightened sense of play.

COLLAGE

I started with a Chinese newspaper I picked up while getting takeout the night before. Then I added a band of image paper from a software flyer and made a ribbon of folded gold-foil paper.

This was a baby present, so I added 2 items that might persist in his room: a toy dinosaur and a personalized twig. I glued them on lightly, with a red square placed diamond-wise to feature the green dinosaur.

Photography by Garry McLeod

RIBBON WEAVE

Place the object between 2 boards. The gift must be suited to this. It could be a small, flat gift box, or it could be a flat object. In this case it was a wooden Christmas ornament that had flat, parallel surfaces. The 2 boards don't have to be wood planks, as shown here. You could use pieces of framer's mat board, or some other beautiful material.

If you look at the left side of the gift, you'll see that the edge of the hidden gift is wrapped in gold ribbon. The ribbon is the same width as the gift itself, an admittedly demanding requirement, but you could simply give the gift a tissue wrap to solve that.

Tape the red and black ribbons onto the backboard, and begin winding and weaving the ribbons. When done, tape the 2 ends onto the backboard. I made a large label on the computer and double-taped it to the messy backside of the package.

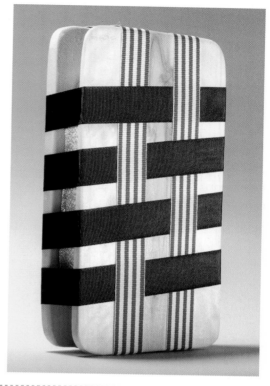

THE OUTER WRAP

The collage is made of brochure and flyer fragments that came in the mail. The "bow" is made of thick white paper strips glue-gunned in place. A ring of fat cord, taken from a shopping bag, is glued around the base of the bow; it pushes the white strips up. The label was made on my computer.

COLLAGE: INNOVATION

Achieve a new look and feel with this wrap. Start with a brown wrap, and attach black paper panels on the front and sides, leaving brown paper peeking through. This alone is a new and useful wrapping tactic you can explore on later packages.

I decided to push it further by adding veils of plastic packing wrap. The first is yellow and forms the vertical band on the right. Then I added a second horizontal band in red. The label, in bright red with gold paint marker, obeys the square composition in shape and placement.

TISSUE BURRITO

Roll it up in tissue. Cut the ends with scissors to create a fringe. Gold, frilly ribbon brightens up and completes the wrap.

BROWN WRAP

This wrap relies on the contrast of rough, brown industrial paper with white gauze ribbon. I had saved this ribbon with the bow intact; the wrap artist saves time by conserving. The label was made with computer-label paper; the image was from our homemade Christmas card.

John Boak is an artist living in Colorado. A graduate of Yale, he is a painter, sculptor, and designer. He exhibits with the William Havu Gallery in Denver.

FOAM WRAP

First wrap the gift in red tissue. Then wrap it in green packing foam, holding it together with red tinsel-trimmed ribbon. Make a quick-glued bow of the same material, and finish it with a trinket like this small wooden hemisphere. This wrap has charm and a sense of humor.

MUMMY WRAP

This wrap is best for oddly shaped gifts with no box. I started with a roll of crepe paper I had left over from a birthday party. Wind it around the gift until it is well covered. This makes for an amusing unwrap. I sealed both ends of the wrap with round stickers from my ongoing collection of random stickers.

BIG-HANDLE BOW

Some wraps are created for entertainment value. I wrapped this one in red shopping-bag paper. After I put on the shiny ribbon, I had the idea of using the bag's twisted-paper handles as a bower, glue-gunned in place, to hold the label.

➕ For more ideas and inspiration, go to boakart.com/wrap/wrapart.html

Flexagons

 Flex your mathematics by folding this multi-layered card.
BY LAURIE COUGHLIN

Invented by Arthur H. Stone in 1939, flexagons are mathematical, multi-layered objects composed of folded paper strips. They usually take the form of a square or hexagon, and there are several variations on the type of flexing and number of faces. When a flexagon is flexed, a new face is revealed. Flexing is similar to folding, but it's not a static motion where there is a beginning and ending point; it's a fluid and continuous forward and backward motion. For our project, we're going to create a standard square flexagon, known as a tetraflexagon, which will reveal 2 new faces.

YOU WILL NEED: Scissors, glue stick, this magazine (or paper and a printer)

TO MAKE THE FLEXAGON

1. First, cut out both of the L-shaped strips on the opposite page. Note that they're double-sided. (If you'd rather not chop up your magazine, you can go to craftzine.com/05/flexagon and print the same images from there, then glue the sides together, back to back, to match the magazine.)
2. Next, lay them horizontally, so that the tallest side is on your left. (The text on side B-1 will be upside down.)
3. Starting from the left, fold over to the right. Repeat.
4. Repeat Step 3 with second strip.

 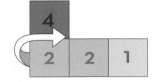 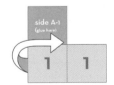

5. Add glue to gray A-1 and B-1 tabs.
6. Line up tabs A-1 with A-2 and tabs B-1 and B-2. Press firmly on each square. Wait 2 minutes before attempting to flex your flexagon.

 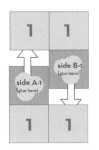 

Illustrations by Laurie Coughlin

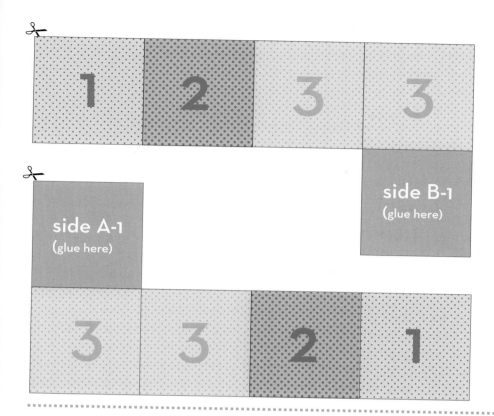

TO FLEX YOUR FLEXAGON

Remember that this is a fluid, rotating motion.

1. Begin with face 1 (pink) facing you.

2. Push both the right and left sides downward. The profile should look like a mountain peak.

3. The first new face, face 2 (blue), will be revealed from the center of the flexagon; with your thumbs, open it up like a book.

4. Repeat Step 2 to reveal face 3 (yellow, second new face).

5. Return to face 1 by reversing the fluid movement. You will be flexing the outside edges toward the center. The profile should look like a V-shape.

NOTE: A second method of returning to the starting point is by flipping the flexagon over so that face 4 is facing you and flexing it twice. Then flip it over once more and face 1 will be facing you.

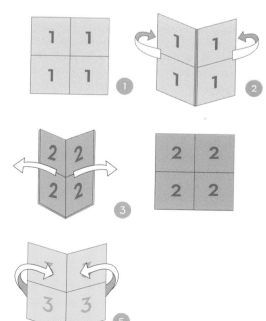

✂

| 2 | 1 | 4 | side B-2 |

| 4 |

| 4 |

| side A-2 | 4 | 1 | 2 |

✂

FLEXAGON HISTORY

In 1939, Arthur H. Stone, a Princeton University graduate, was folding strips of paper for his amusement when he created the first flexagon. But it was not until 14 years later that the general public took notice of this fun, mathematical paper-folding puzzle. In 1956, Martin Gardner wrote an article on flexagons, which was published in *Scientific American* magazine. Since then, every generation has rediscovered this wonderful paper object.

RESOURCES:

History: eighthsquare.com/flexhistory.html

The Magic of Flexagons: Paper Curiosities to Cut Out & Make by David Mitchell

Hexaflexagons and Other Mathematical Diversions: The First Scientific American *Book of Puzzles and Games* by Martin Gardner

Flexagons Inside Out by Les Pook

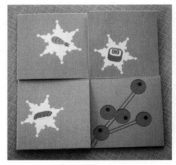

The author's flexagon card illustrates the passing of time while catching snowflakes in your mouth. The third face reveals a penguin pretending that snowflakes are a tasty sushi treat.

Laurie Coughlin is the designer and owner of Motormouthpress, LLC, a stationery and greeting card company that specializes in food themes and cards that double as mementos. Check out her Penguin Flexagon card at motormouthpress.com.

Photography by Sam Murphy

Craft: PROJECTS

One of most personalized gifts you can give is a keepsake quilt, and here, with modern embellishments like photo images, you can create an heirloom quilt that feels fresh. You can also freshen up your wardrobe with a personalized pattern to sew your own party dress, followed by a sleek skirt made from your favorite T-shirt. Finally, check it all out with a playful op-art mirror — if you dare!

MODERN
HEIRLOOM
QUILT

By Susan Beal

PERSONALIZE A QUILT WITH PHOTO TRANSFERS, GOCCO PRINTS, AND HAND EMBROIDERY.

Since quilting has such a long and venerable history, making a keepsake quilt seemed like the perfect way to celebrate my second wedding anniversary, especially since cotton is the traditional gift. Though log cabin quilting often uses small center squares with narrow surrounding strips, I wanted to make something more open and modern, in an array of colors. I kept the centers and panels large enough to show the prints and patterns of some of my favorite fabrics.

I used my sewing machine to piece, quilt, and bind the quilt, but I embellished the squares by hand to add a personal touch. Using photo transfer images, Gocco prints, embroidery in my own handwriting, and vintage button embellishments made it very us.

» The log cabin quilt design gained popularity in the United States during Abraham Lincoln's presidency. Lincoln himself grew up in a log cabin.

» American pioneer women saved old letters and newspaper clippings to use as patterns for popular paper quilting. Later, the paper found between old quilts became a diary of pioneer life.

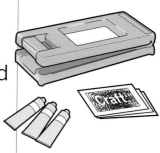

» The word *gocco* in Japanese means "make-believe play," used to learn common rules and general knowledge.

Susan Beal is a writer and designer. She co-wrote *Super Crafty: Over 75 Amazing How-to Projects*, and her jewelry, skirt kits, and writing can be found at susanstars.com and westcoastcrafty.com.

Photograph by Sam Murphy; illustrations by Tim Lillis

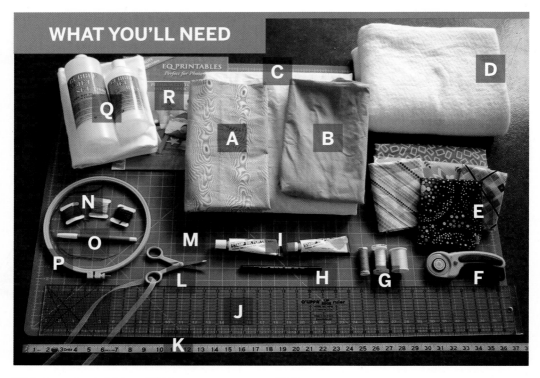

WHAT YOU'LL NEED

[A] 3yds wood-grain fabric

[B] ¼yd blue or other solid fabric for printing

[C] 2yds unbleached cotton muslin (108" wide) or 4yds 54"-wide

[D] Thin batting at least 85"×85"

[E] 40–50 prints and patterns of your choice in remnants or fat quarters

[F] Rotary cutter

[G] All-purpose and cotton threads in off-white, and all-purpose thread in brown to match the wood grain

[H] Gocco pen

[I] Fabric inks

[J] 36" quilting rule

[K] Measuring tape

[L] Sharp fabric scissors

[M] Cutting mat

[N] Embroidery floss in colors of your choice

[O] Fabric marking pen

[P] Embroidery needle and embroidery hoop

For photo-transfer squares
[Q] Bubble Jet Set fabric treatment and white fabric

[R] Freezer paper or printable fabric sheets

For Gocco-printed squares
Gocco printer with fabric stamp. For a Gocco printer

and supplies, try ebay.com or paper-source.com.

[NOT SHOWN]
QuiltTak baster and tabs

Sewing machine

Iron and ironing board

Straight pins

White sheet

1" bias tape maker

Inkjet printer and paper

This finished quilt measures 80"×80" and includes 25 log cabin squares, each 13" and using 2 different fabrics (or 1 photo/print and 1 fabric). I also bordered each print with thinner wood-grain strips for a picture-frame effect, and chose neutral, off-white cotton as the surrounding fabric so the colors could really shine. For the back, I made 2 long, patchwork panels in the same fabrics and placed them running horizontally across for simplicity. Make the quilt your own: use all photos or Gocco prints, make each square identical, change the proportions ... it's up to you!

NOTE: Throughout this project, you'll sew with a ¼" seam allowance unless otherwise mentioned. Always backstitch at the beginning and end of a seam to keep it strong and reinforced. When building the squares, keep your iron handy because you'll be pressing each seam as you go. For piecing and binding, use all-purpose sewing thread, and for quilting, use the natural-colored cotton quilting thread.

Photography by Susan Beal

⏩ STITCH A CUSTOM, MODERN QUILT

Time: 1 Month   Complexity: Medium

1. CREATE THE CENTERS

1a. Using a rotary cutter and quilting ruler, cut out sixteen 6" squares as your fabric centers. I chose a mix of vintage and new prints in 4 different color families. Remember that you'll lose ¼" on each side to the seam, so your finished center will be 5½"×5½".

NOTE: The following 2 steps are flexible. If you don't have a Gocco printer, simply make 9 photos for printing, rather than 5. Or if you're passionate about Gocco, you can make 9 Gocco squares and skip the photos. Or skip the next 2 steps completely and cut out 25 squares rather than 16 in Step 1a. Mix it up as you please.

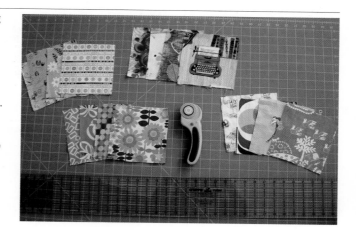

1b. Cut four 6" squares of your solid fabric for Gocco printing. Create the image you want to print on paper. I decided to make a map of Oregon that I could embellish with our favorite places, so I traced it on paper using a Gocco pen, burned a screen, and printed 4 identical map images in green and brown. (For complete Gocco fabric printing instructions, see craftzine.com/go/gocco.)

1c. Prepare 5 hi-res (300 dpi or better) photographs for printing, at 5½"×5½" or the size you want them to be. I left mine smaller and bordered by white space so I could embroider there. Now use your white fabric and Bubble Jet Set (or a commercially prepared photo-transfer fabric) and an inkjet printer to print them, following the label instructions carefully to prepare and wash them. When ready, cut these down to 6" squares as well. You should now have 25 center squares total now.

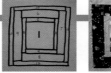

2. BUILD THE SQUARES

2a. Begin cutting long strips of wood-grain fabric, each 1½" wide, from selvedge to fold. You'll need about 28" for the inner frame and about 50" for the outer frame of each square. Trim all the selvedge edges so no white shows.

2b. Take your first center and place a wood-grain strip against it, flush with one edge and right sides facing (as shown). For this project, it doesn't matter which side you start with, and you can hold the 2 fabrics together or use straight pins. Stitch them together with the center square on top and the strip you're joining underneath, using a medium stitch length on your machine. Cut the extra length away at the edge so it's square and neat, and press the seam toward the center so it looks like the picture on the right.

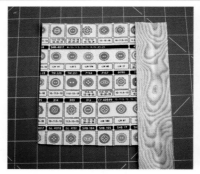 

2c. Working clockwise, overlap the first wood-grain strip with a second one, and stitch. Cut and press it the same way. Repeat with a third and a fourth strip, and then press all seams toward the center again.

2d. Use the technique in Steps 2a–2c to make 24 more squares (for 25 total). To save time, you can work on them in batches: join all the first strips, then press them all toward the centers, add all the second strips, press them all, and so on.

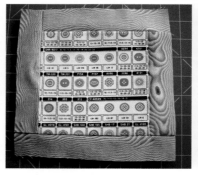 

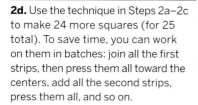

2e. Cut 2½"-wide strips of each of your 25 contrast prints, about 40" long (which could be broken up into several lengths if you're using fat quarters or remnants). Add strips of the contrast fabric to each side of the square in the same way you attached the wood-grain strips. Save all leftover strips of fabric.

2f. Once all 25 squares have the second round of strips attached, you can add a last round of wood-grain fabric to each one, just as you did the first time. Press all seams toward the center.

3. EMBELLISH THE SQUARES

3a. I embroidered each of the photo and Gocco-print squares with my own designs after adding the first round of patterned fabric strips. For the Gocco maps, I chose 4 of my favorite places in Oregon and hand-sewed a star button to mark each one. I used a fabric marking pen to hand-write each name, then threaded a needle with 2 strands of embroidery floss, doubled it, and began following the pattern with a simple running stitch. For the Portland square, I added 2 flowers using simple loops and a running-stitch vine, then hand-wrote the name underneath and embroidered that too.

3b. For the photos, I wrote a phrase describing each one on the white space next to it, and embroidered them all in running stitch. I also added a few vintage buttons here and there to decorate them.

4. MAKE THE QUILT TOP AND BACK

4a. Set a white sheet out on the floor and place your quilt squares on it, 5 across and 5 down. Arrange them as you like, so you have an interesting mix of colors that aren't too jarring or too similar to neighbors. I chose to place my photo squares in the center and on each side (where the 12, 3, 6, and 9 positions would be on a clock face), and place the Gocco squares between them. When you're happy with your design, take a quick photo to remember the placement.

4b. Begin cutting 2½"-wide strips of the neutral muslin fabric (you'll need about 9 strips, each 108" long and 2½" wide) for joining the squares. Working with 1 column of squares, take the first one and join a strip of muslin to the bottom edge, just as you did with the wood-grain and patterned fabrics. Cut it off at the edge. Now join the second square to the other long edge of muslin and press both seams toward the centers. You'll have 2 squares joined by one 2"-wide strip of off-white fabric.

4c. Join the next 3 squares the same way, so that you have a long column of 5 squares in a row. Repeat with the other 4 columns of 5, and then join each column with a long strip of muslin the same way. Finish the top by adding long strips to each side — it should now measure approximately 80"×80". As your quilt grows in size, keep a chair to the left of your sewing machine, where the weight of your quilt can rest while you sew.

4d. To make the quilt back, begin piecing your 2½"-wide fabric scraps from Step 2e in a random mix of long and short lengths, so you create two 82" strips of patchworked prints.

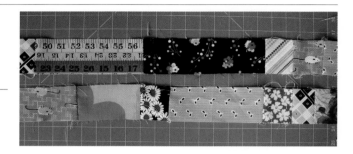

4e. Cut 3 pieces of muslin: one 52"×82", one 2½"×82", and one 24"×82". Piece them together from smaller sections if necessary.

4f. Construct the back of the quilt in this order: join the top edge of the first patchwork strip to a long edge of the 52"×82" piece, right sides facing, and then join the 2½"-wide strip to the bottom edge of the patchwork strip. Now join the second patchwork strip to the lower edge of the muslin in the same way. Finish by adding the 24"×82" piece along the bottom edge and then press the whole thing, ironing all seams toward the patchwork strip center.

5. BASTE AND QUILT

5a. Place your quilt back, wrong side up, on a floor or large cutting table. Add the batting on top of it, smoothing it out flat, and then place the quilt top above that, right side up. The batting should extend out a few inches on each side, and the back will be a bit larger than the front.

5b. Make sure that the quilt top is centered over the back and that both are lying flat. Working from one end, begin basting it with the QuilTak tool, following the instructions carefully. Baste it every 5" or 6", and after finishing the first area, roll it toward the center and keep basting the next section.

5c. Use a simple stitch-in-the-ditch pattern that traces the outer seam of each of the wood-grain squares. Thread your machine with cotton quilting thread and begin quilting at one of the outside edges, following the seam as you go. You can either stitch around all 4 sides of 1 square at a time, or follow the outer edge of each of the 5 squares in a straight line in a single column, then the inner edge of each of the 5, and so on.

5d. To quilt more than one edge in a row, backstitch at the end of each wood-grain panel; to save time, you can lift your presser foot up and reposition it at the next panel along a straight line, instead of stopping, clipping the thread, and starting again. You'll just need to snip all the thread loops on the quilt after each long seam.

5e. As you move toward the center, roll the quilt up so it fits neatly inside the sewing machine arm, and drape the outer section over a chair or table to your left so it doesn't pull your stitching to the side. Finish quilting all 50 inner and outer wood-grain squares; you can easily look on the back to see if you've missed any.

5f. Lay the quilt facedown and remove all the QuilTak basting tabs with scissors (they're easiest to see on the back). Now turn it over so it's right side up and use your rotary cutter to cut away the excess batting and back, moving the cutting mat underneath the quilt as you go. Then stitch around the perimeter of the quilt, ⅜" away from the edge.

6. BIND THE QUILT

6a. Make custom bias tape to bind your quilt in the same wood-grain fabric as your squares. For an 80"×80" quilt, you'll need a total of about 335" of binding (almost 28'). Cut 2"-wide strips of fabric, selvedge to selvedge, and cut off the white edges as before. Join 2 strips at a right angle, right sides facing, machine-stitch them at a 45° angle, and clip the excess fabric away. Press the seam to one side.

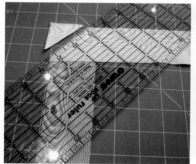

6b. Continue joining until you have enough length to cover the perimeter of the quilt. You may want to store it in a zip-lock bag so it doesn't tangle. Now feed the end into the bias tape maker and ease it through the narrower opening so that it folds itself neatly, pressing it flat with your iron as you go. When you've finished a few feet of bias tape, fold it in half so the raw edges meet inside and iron it securely flat.

6c. Bind the quilt with your handmade bias tape. (For detailed instructions on binding your quilt, see craftzine.com/05/heirloomquilt.)

I highly recommend the excellent "One-Step Binding" section of Weeks Ringle and Bill Kerr's *Modern Quilt Workshop* for clear, easy-to-follow instructions. That's it! Sign your name and embellish as you desire.

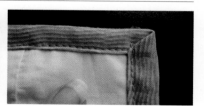

FINISH

PARTY DRESS

By Christine Haynes
and Kent Bell

SEW A FESTIVE DRESS FROM YOUR OWN CUSTOM, REUSABLE PATTERN.

➤➤ Picture this: You're at a cocktail party and your new dress is turning heads and winning compliments. Imagine the pride you'll feel when you reveal your big secret: "Oh, this little thing? I made it yesterday."

Now imagine being able to make several versions of the same dress in different fabrics, lengths, and variations, and never having to remeasure or recalculate. Just lay down your custom-made pattern, cut your fabric, and finish it in record time.

With this project, you'll learn to make a sewing pattern and a closet full of garments to fit the one and only you.

» Audrey Hepburn's Givenchy dress from the 1961 movie *Breakfast at Tiffany's* sold for more than £467,200 (over $800,000) at a 2006 Christie's auction in London.

» Diane von Furstenberg's wrap dress emerged on the fashion scene in the early 70s and is still popular today.

» The term *LBD* is short for "little black dress," the essential piece of clothing that all women should have in their wardrobes.

With their company, Twospace, Christine Haynes and Kent Bell use sewing machines and other equipment nearly every day to create modern, casual clothing and jewelry. See the fruits of their labor at twospace.com.

Photography by Kent Bell and Christine Haynes; illustrations by Tim Lillis

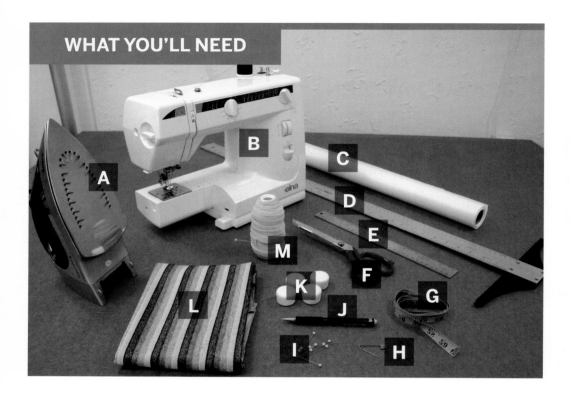

WHAT YOU'LL NEED

[A] Iron

[B] Sewing machine

[C] Roll of craft paper

[D] T square

[E] Ruler

[F] Scissors

[G] Tape measure

[H] Safety pin

[I] Straight pins

[J] Sharp-point pencil

[K] Weights

[L] Fabric

[M] Elastic ½"-wide

▶▶ CREATE A PATTERN FOR A FUN DRESS WITH OPTIONS

Time: 3 Hours Complexity: Medium

1. MEASURE YOUR BODY AND CALCULATE YOUR NUMBERS

When making a pattern, it's always easier to make an item where the left and right sides of the body are a mirror image. When this is the case, you only need to make half of the pattern, as you can line up your pattern piece along the fold of your fabric and cut both sides at once. This is not only easier, it also guarantees that your creation will be perfectly symmetrical. In this dress, the front and back panels are also the same. So you only have to make one quarter of the dress, place it on the fold, and cut it out twice.

1a. To draw the first line on the pattern, you first need to measure your bust and apply a little math. To measure your bust, place the tape under your arms, around the fullest part of your chest, and shoulder blades. Be sure to keep the tape measure level across your back.

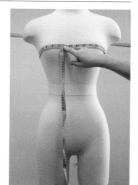

Now for the math: Take your bust measurement and add 6". This is to add fullness in the dress. You can adjust this number based on how full you'd like it to be. Now take that number and divide it by 4, as the pattern piece is only ¼ of the dress. This is measurement A.

EXAMPLE: For our sample dress, the bust measurement was 34".
    34 + 6 = 40
    40 ÷ 4 = 10
    A = 10"

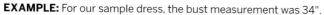

1b. Measure your hips by wrapping the tape around the fullest part of your body at the top of your legs, with your feet together and the tape parallel to the floor. Take your hip measurement and add 14" for fullness, then divide that number by 4. This is measurement B.

EXAMPLE: For our dress, the hip measurement was 35".
    35 + 14 = 49
    49 ÷ 4 = 12.25
    B = 12¼"

❋ **TIP: If your hips are smaller than your bust, insert your bust measurement into this formula to get measurement B. This ensure's a nice flare for your dress.**

1c. Measure your waist at your natural waistline, just above your navel. This is measurement C.

1d. Beginning just under your armpit, decide how long you would like your dress to be. Short and sassy? Long and elegant? Be careful not to bend over too much while taking this measurement. The tape measure will bend with you, making your dress longer than you really want. Your preferred length is measurement D.

1e. Lastly, measure from your bust to your hip along the side of your body. This is measurement E.

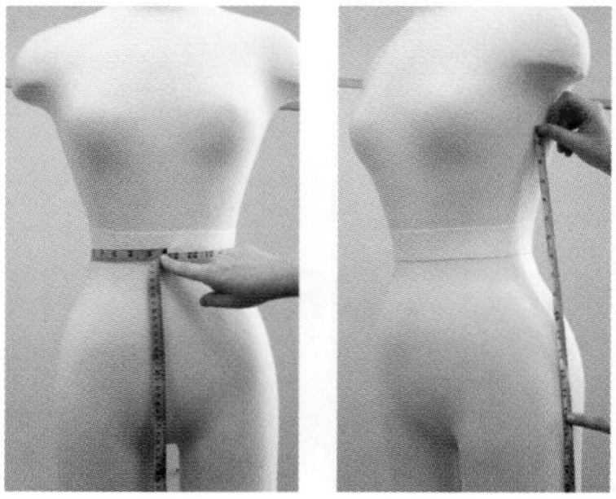

MEASURING TIP: **To get the most accurate measurements, it's best to measure yourself in undergarments only. If you don't have a measuring tape, use a piece of string or ribbon and lay that alongside a ruler. Using a full-length mirror can help you measure lengths down your body without slouching.**

2. MAKE YOUR CUSTOM PATTERN

2a. Roll out your craft paper and weigh down the corners to keep it flat. Align your paper along a square table lengthwise so that the long side of the paper's edge runs along the edge of the table.

2b. Lay your T square down and press the handle along the table's edge to form a 90° angle. Leaving a few inches at the end of the roll as buffer, use a sharp-point pencil to draw a line the length of measurement A.

2c. Starting at line A, measure (down the paper) a distance matching measurement E. This is where line B will begin. Now draw measurement B.

2d. Line your T square up to the endpoints of the A and B lines and mark down measurement D. Begin this line 3" above A so the dress will begin above your bust, and draw down past the hips until you have your desired length.

2e. Using the T square again from the edge of the table, connect the top and bottom endpoints of measurement D to the edge of the paper. This is the top and bottom of your dress.

2f. Following along your outermost pencil marks, use scissors to cut out your pattern. You should now have what looks like half of a pyramid. This is your dress pattern!

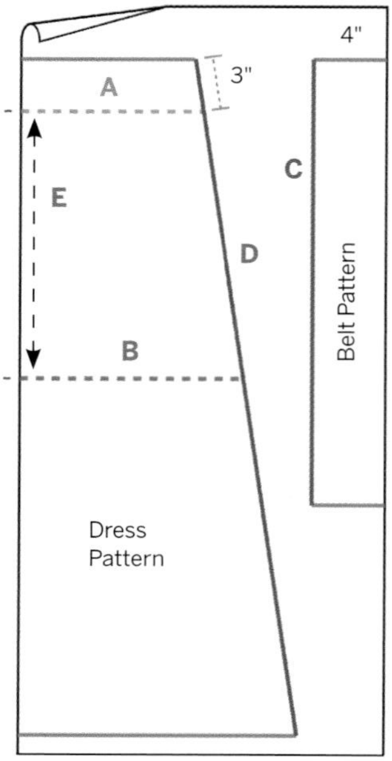

2g. To make the belt, use your T square and mark out the length of measurement C. Measure out your desired width and reconnect the lines to form a rectangle. Don't forget to consider a seam allowance when choosing your width. Ours was cut 4" wide, including a ½" seam allowance.

3. CUT YOUR FABRIC

First you have to choose some fabric. We chose a sparkly silver polyester blend, since it's holiday party season! But you can make this out of just about anything. Cotton prints, stretch jersey, and silks are all good choices, too. And don't forget that your belt can be contrasting as well. So if your dress is made with black and white gingham, a solid red belt would make it sizzle!

3a. Roll out your fabric and fold it in half with selvedges together. Place the long, square edge of your pattern (not the "sloped" side) on the fold. Hold down your pattern with weights so it doesn't move, and cut it out.

3b. Repeat Step 3a to cut out a second dress piece.

3c. Place your belt pattern piece with the short edge on a fold. We chose to change the direction of the stripes for the belt. Cut out 2 of these. You should end up with 4 pattern pieces: 2 identical dress pyramids and 2 identical belt rectangles.

4. SEW YOUR DRESS

4a. If your dress fabric will fray in the washing machine, use a zigzag stitch to finish off the inside seam edges first. Most cotton fabrics will fray, but polyesters and jerseys will not.

4b. Line up your 2 dress pieces, right sides together, and pin in place. Using a ½" seam allowance, sew the 2 sides of your dress together.

4c. Heat up your iron and press your side seams flat, then press your hem up and stitch. Fold down the top of the dress 1" and press.

4d. Starting at a side seam, stitch the top flap down, leaving a 1" opening unstitched, to insert the elastic. Using ½"-wide elastic, measure a piece of elastic the width of your bust measurement. Be careful not to pull on the elastic while measuring it — it's stretchy! Attach a large safety pin about ¼" from the end of the elastic, and insert the pinned elastic into the open hole in the bust casing. Using the pin as a guide to pull on, feed the elastic all the way through. Be careful not to twist the elastic in the process.

4e. Pin the elastic to hold. Slip the dress on and adjust the elastic to a length that will keep the dress on, yet still be comfortable to wear. It's usually about 6" or so smaller than your bust measurement.

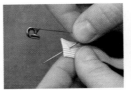

4f. Trim the extra elastic off, leaving enough to overlap about 1". Use a zigzag stitch to sew the 2 pieces together, going over the same area a few times to secure it.

4g. Pull the elastic into the hole, and then stitch the hole closed, making sure you don't stitch into the elastic.

4h. To make the belt, stitch right sides together along both long sides, using a ½" seam allowance. Then turn the belt right side out and press. Fold down the ends about ½" into the inside and press again. Now stitch the ends closed.

FINISH

VARIATIONS ON YOUR CUSTOM DRESS

The reason you go through the bother of making the pattern and doing all the math in the first place is because the pattern you now have is the basis for many other garments. Here are suggestions on how to use this pattern in different ways, for a wardrobe of handmade goodness.

1. To make a skirt:
Follow all the same steps as in making the dress, but when inserting elastic into the casing, adjust the elastic to fit your waist or hip, depending on where you want to wear it. If your hips are too large to fit the existing pattern, fold down the top of the pattern until it fits your hip measurement. Then just adjust the length.

2. To add a halter:
Use the same techniques for making the belt, but make 2 straps for a halter in your desired width. After sewing the ends closed, pin them to the front of your dress at a slight angle toward your neck. They will buckle at the top of your dress if you sew them perpendicular to the dress. After you pin them on, try on the dress and adjust to fit. Stitch the straps just above and below the elastic, and tie the ends around the back of your neck.

3. To add shoulder straps:
Make 2 straps in your desired width. Place them perpendicular to the top of the dress about 5" from the side seam. Pin them to the front of the bust and sew in place. Pin the straps to the back of the dress and adjust to find the right fit. Cut off excess strap length and sew to the back of the dress.

4. To add shoulder ties:
Make 4 straps, approximately 22" long. Then pin them to the front and back of the dress on each side, about 5" from the side seam. Sew in place and tie the straps at the top of your shoulders into sweet little bows.

5. To add a bottom ruffle:
Ruffles are usually the width of the hem, plus half of that same distance. To add a bottom ruffle, measure the bottom width of your dress. Cut that number in half, and add it to the original number.

For example, if the bottom width is 36", you'd add 36 to 18 for a total of 54". On your craft paper, measure out 54" wide by the desired length of your ruffle long. Don't forget to add some length for the seam allowance at the top and the hem at the bottom. Cut out 2 of these, one for the front and one for the back. Sew the pieces together at the short ends, with right sides together. Baste along the top edge and gather to match the width of your skirt hem. Pin ruffle to skirt with right sides facing together. Stitch in place and hem.

6. Belts:
You can use the belt in this project, and wear it at your waist, at your hip, or under your bust for an empire-waist dress. You can also wear the dress without a belt at all, or you can add a belt you bought somewhere else. Belts are also great for covering the elastic waist when wearing the dress as a skirt.

T-SKIRT

By Eileen Kirkham

MOD A T-SHIRT INTO A SLEEK, FORM-FITTING JUMPER.

▶▶ They're everywhere. Comfortable, beautiful, bold, subtle, controversial, flippant: T-shirts! Starting with a simple tee, you can make an endless and completely unique wardrobe of skirts, jumpers, halters … the only limit is your imagination.

Re-use buttons, sleeves, collars, pockets from your old jeans, parachute buckles from that old backpack; try to look at everything as a possible embellishment or integral part of a new garment.

An easy first project in T-shirt repurposing is a simple jumper. Depending on your sewing skills, and the degree of embellishment you decide on, you can whip up a T-skirt or jumper in less than a day.

» In British English, a jumper dress is known as a pinafore, or "pinny" for short.

» Actor James Dean made the T-shirt a symbol of rebellious youth in the 1955 movie, *Rebel Without a Cause*.

» In the 80s, T-shirts with bold slogans were popular like this "Frankie Say Relax" shirt from the band Frankie Goes to Hollywood.

Eileen Kirkham learned to sew by watching her mom try to keep her five leggy girls stylishly clothed. She's sewn lingerie, jeans, swimwear, and upholstery. Her current passion is creating T-skirts and sinfully soft blankets.

Photograph by Gabriela Hasbun at My Friend Joe, Sebastopol, Calif.; illustrations by Tim Lillis

WHAT YOU'LL NEED

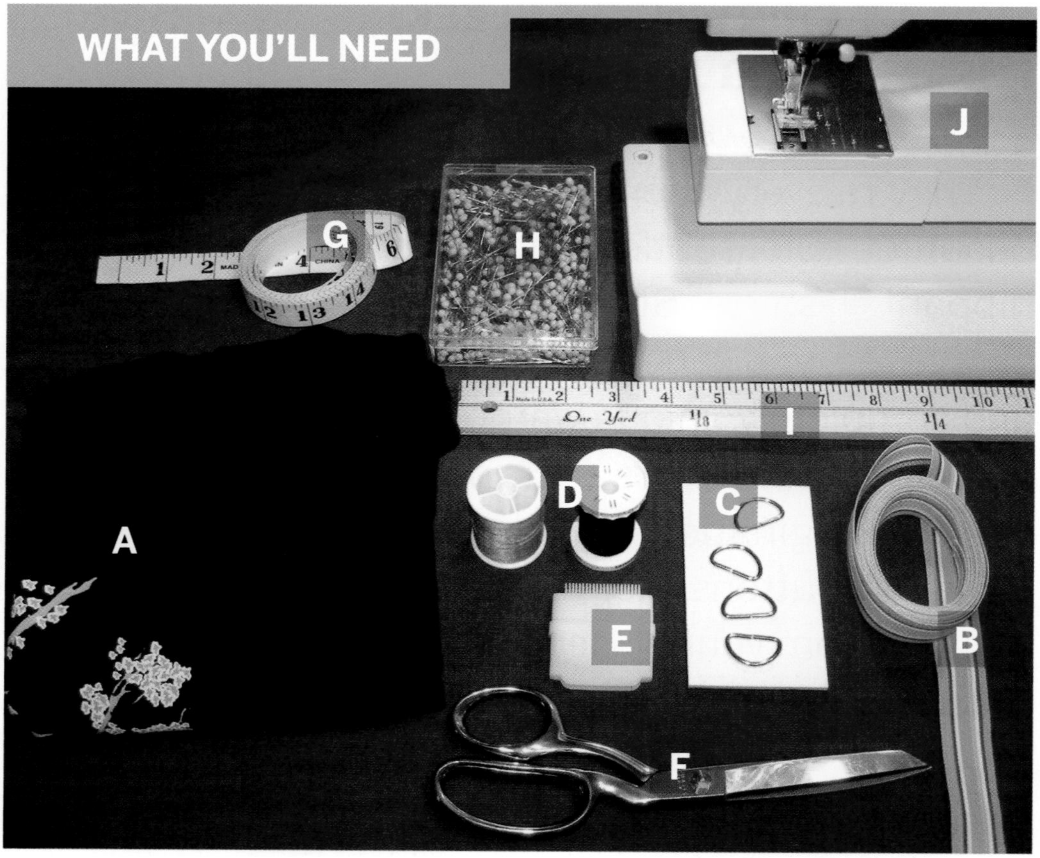

[A] T-shirt, large or XL
new or used

[B] 3yds of 1"–3" wide
double-face ribbon, or 6yds
of single-face ribbon You
can use all one kind of ribbon,
or use 3yds each of coordi-
nating/contrasting ribbon in
the same width.

[C] D-rings (4) to fit the
width of the ribbon you use

[D] Thread

[E] Tailor's chalk

[F] Scissors

[G] Measuring tape

[H] Straight pins

[I] Yardstick

[J] Sewing machine

Serger (optional)

Photography by Eileen Kirkham

▶▶ TRANSFORM AN OLD T-SHIRT INTO A NEW T-SKIRT

Time: 1–2 Days Complexity: Easy

1. MEASURE YOURSELF

You'll want to measure your waist and hips. Then measure from the lower edge of your bra to the point where you want the hem to fall — at your knees or just below them. Choose a T-shirt that is 1" or 2" wider than the widest point of your hip measurement. Then hold the T-shirt against yourself, just below your bust, to make certain you have a shirt that will reach the length you want.

✳ **TIP: Measure yourself, then the tee, to be sure you have the right size tee for your body. Bigger tees and extra fabric are always easier to work with.**

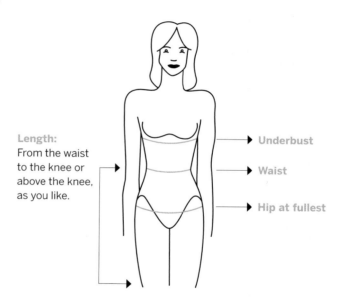

Length:
From the waist to the knee or above the knee, as you like.

▶ Underbust

▶ Waist

▶ Hip at fullest

2. PREPARE TEE FOR RESHAPING AND PEG THE HEM

2a. Turn the T-shirt inside out. With your hand inside the sleeve and your fingertips supporting the body of the T-shirt, start snipping the T-shirt as close as possible to the serged sleeve seam, going all around the sleeve, with the serged edge remaining on the sleeve. When you finish, you should have a smooth, raw armhole. Repeat on the opposite sleeve.

2b. Moving from the armhole toward the neckline, cut the shoulder seam, cutting as close as possible to the seam, continuing straight through the ribbing. Repeat this on the opposite shoulder. The shoulders should both have raw edges, and you should be able to lay them flat.

2c. With the shirt lying flat, create the pegged pencil skirt shape by marking a line from the top of the hip to the hemline. The degree of pegging is up to you. I usually make the width of the skirt at the hem 3"–6" less than the fullest part of the hips.

3. ■ FIT THE SKIRT

You can choose one of the following 3 methods to fit your skirt. Although you may get the perfect fit the first time, be prepared to make a couple of tweaks.

Method 1 The easiest way to fit the skirt is to slip the prepared T-shirt on yourself, inside out, and pin the skirt to fit. Be sure to fit the skirt with the ribbing in a high-waist position. After pinning the length of the skirt from high waist to hem, run your tailor's chalk beside the pin line on each side, front and back. In case you need to remove some pins, you'll still have a seam line guide to re-pin.

Carefully remove the skirt. Using the basting stitch on your machine (4–6 stitches per inch), sew the new side seams for your skirt. Turn it right side out and try it on to check your fit. Baste the adjustment. Repeat this step until you have the fit you desire.

When the tweaking is finished, sew the side seam with a normal stitch of 2.5–3 stitches per inch. If you have trouble with this method, you might enlist the help of a friend. Pinning is sometimes easier when done by a second pair of hands.

NOTE: If adjustments need to be made, turn the skirt inside out, slip it back on, and chalk mark what adjustments are needed. I use tailor's chalk, but you can also use pins.

Method 2 Slip the prepared T-shirt on a dress form, inside out, and pin the skirt to fit the form you have set with your measurements. As in Method 1, be sure to fit the skirt with the ribbing in a high-waist position. After pinning the skirt as far as you can down the side, run your tailor's chalk beside the pin line on each side, front and back.

Carefully remove the skirt and lay it flat. Using a yardstick, find the center front of your skirt hem and tick with chalk. Next, determine the width you want. I peg all the pencil skirts I make, meaning the width of the skirt at the hem is 2"–4" narrower than the fullest measurement of the hips. Mark the desired width at the hem. Next, position the yardstick at the last pin on the hip down to the widest point of your hem and chalk a line beside the stick. Repeat this on the opposite side, and pin.

Baste the seams you have pinned (4–6 stitches per inch) and the new side seams for your skirt. Turn it right side out and try it on to check your fit. If further adjustments need to be made, turn inside out, slip the skirt back on, and chalk mark what adjustments are needed. I use tailor's chalk, but you can also pin. Baste the adjustment. Repeat this step until you have the fit you desire. When finished tweaking, sew the side seam with a normal stitch of 2.5–3 stitches per inch.

Method 3 Trace a skirt that fits the way you like. Simply turn the skirt inside out, lay it on the T-shirt (which is also inside out), and trace the sides of the skirt. Remember, this T-skirt will be high-waisted, so you may want to position the waist of the skirt about 3" below the ribbing of the T-shirt at center front.

Baste (4–6 stitches per inch) using the chalk line as your stitching guide. Baste-stitch to the waistline of the T-skirt, slip it on, and check the fit. Be sure to also fit the remaining high waist. Baste-stitch and fit until you have the desired fit. When you're satisfied, sew a permanent seam at 2.5–3 stitches per inch. Trim the seam allowances down to about ½" to ¼" from the side seams, and serge or zigzag to finish the edge.

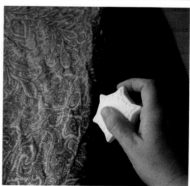

4. PREPARE AND ATTACH THE SUSPENDERS

At this point, you should have a high-waisted skirt that is form-fitting (to whatever degree you desire). If you have chosen to use double-faced satin ribbon, you can skip ahead to Step 4b.

4a. Gather 6yds of single-face ribbon. If you choose to use only one type of ribbon, cut your ribbon into 4 even pieces — each should be about 56" long. If using 2 different types of ribbon, cut each type into 2 pieces 56" long. Next, place 2 pieces of ribbon wrong sides together and sew along both lengthwise edges to make two 56" pieces of ribbon that are different on each side. Take each piece of ribbon, place a pin 6" from the end of each piece, and determine which side you want facing up, or showing, during normal wear.

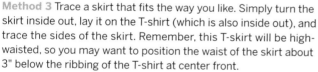

4b. To prepare the edge of the skirt for the ribbon, serge the raw edge that starts at the front, parallel to the ribbing section, continues around the underarm edge of the skirt, and ends parallel to the ribbing at the back. If you don't have a serger, you can zigzag stitch this same path, or eyeball about a ¼" edge.

4c. Start pinning the ribbon to the inside edge of the skirt, starting at the 6" mark you pinned earlier, and using the ¼" stitching as a pinning guide.

With the wrong sides together, pin the lower edge of the ribbon to the edge of the skirt so that the lower edge of the ribbon extends just below the ¼" edge stitching. Repeat on the opposite side.

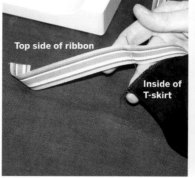
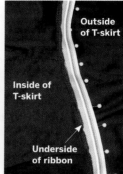

4d. Stitch the ribbon along the pinned edge, right side up and as neatly as possible. This is going to be on the top edge of your finished skirt. Again, repeat on the opposite side.

4e. Fold the ribbon to the outside of the jumper and pin in place. Stitch along the new lower edge of the ribbon. Topstitch ¼" from the top edge of the ribbon for a flatter fold. Repeat on the opposite side. Depending on the degree of drape and crosswise stretch, some ribbon will require a small dart under the arm to lay completely flat. If necessary, take a tiny tuck and topstitch each side of the dart, from the top edge to the point. The shoulder straps and lower straps are in place!

5. ATTACH YOUR D-RINGS

Turning your attention back to the front, you're ready to position the straps so you can attach your D-rings. Two D-rings per strap are needed.

5a. Slip the shoulder strap ribbon through the 2 rings so that the rings lie over the bust, but hang 2" above the lower straps. Pin the ribbon snuggly against the positioned D-rings and check the fit by running the lower straps through them. Once the proper length is definitely determined, trim the excess ribbon away from the pinned ribbon, leaving a 1½" tail.

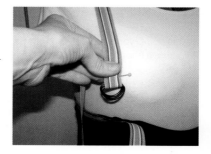

5b. With the D-rings still pinned, tuck the ribbon tail under twice, so the raw edge of the ribbon is folded to the inside — about ¾" once, then once again. Pin the fold and stitch the folded edge to permanently attach the D-rings. Topstitch again halfway between the D-rings and the folded stitch line. Repeat on opposite side.

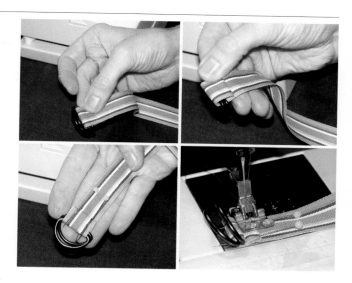

6. ADD YOUR FINISHING STITCHES

6a. The straps will have naturally crisscrossed in back, creating almost a racer back. Once you have a firm fit, you will come back and stitch a triangle to maintain this effect permanently, but pin it for now, in case you need to adjust it.

6b. Slip your jumper on, drawing the straps over your shoulders and running them through the D-rings. Adjust everything and take a peek in the mirror, making sure everything is where you want it to be.

Double-check the back where the straps meet to be certain they lie smoothly. Remove your jumper. Hem the lower straps and sew a triangle tack at the racer-back strap.

FINISH ✕

OPTICAL DELUSIONAL MIRROR

By Matt Maranian

CREATE TRIPPY OP-ART IMAGES THAT CHANGE DEPENDING ON WHERE YOU STAND.

» The "House of Mirrors" attraction typical at most amusement parks has origins in the Palace of Versailles' Hall of Mirrors.

▶▶ This design was inspired by those cheap-o-delic little picture boxes crafted in Mexico, which feature three lurid images of various Catholic saints.

These louvered icons allow the viewer to see one saint from the left and another from the right, by way of a low-end illusion. But since Catholic iconography creeps me out a little, and the last time I went to church Debby Boone had a hit with "You Light Up My Life," I decided to substitute a functional wall mirror and a couple of icons I can stand behind with honest-to-goodness, genuflecting enthusiasm: my favorite Jewish comic, Groucho Marx, and my favorite German singer, Nina Hagen. This mirror was created for an 11"×14" frame using two images placed vertically, but you can modify it to any size.

» The passenger-side car mirror is convex, creating a wider range of view and a false impression that objects are farther away. Hence the disclaimer, "Objects in mirror are closer than they appear."

» Comedian Groucho Marx is one of the most famous icons reproduced in popular culture, from cartoons to commercials to these famous costume glasses.

Matt Maranian is a best-selling writer, designer, and bon vivant whose books include *PAD* and *PAD Parties*. He lives in New England.

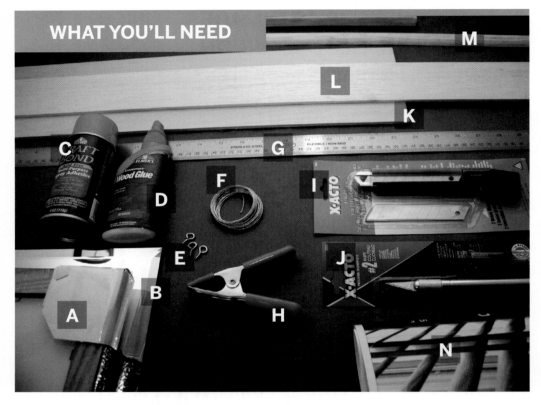

WHAT YOU'LL NEED

[A] 11"×14" picture frame with glass

[B] 11"×14" mirror

[C] Spray mount adhesive

[D] Wood glue

[E] $^{11}/_{16}$" short shank screw eyes (2)

[F] 10lb picture-hanging wire

[G] Metal yardstick

[H] Spring clamps or small vise clamps (2)

[I] Utility knife

[J] Paper cutter or X-Acto knife

[K] $^{3}/_{16}$"×3"×36" balsa wood strips (2)

[L] $^{3}/_{32}$"×3"×36" balsa wood strip

[M] ½" quarter round trim, 24" piece

[N] Images (2), no larger than 10½"×14" ideally printed on photocopy paper rather than thick photo paper

[NOT SHOWN]

1" Clearwood corner trim

Fine sandpaper

Pencil

Miter box and saw

MOD A MIRROR THAT REFLECTS MORE THAN JUST YOU

Time: **2–3 Hours** Complexity: **Easy**

1. PREP THE IMAGE BACKING

Work along the edge of a tabletop or a work surface that you don't mind scratching up.

With a pencil, mark the 1½" center points along the length of the strip of ³⁄₃₂" balsa. Use clamps or a small vise over a metal yardstick positioned down the center marks of the balsa strip. With the metal yardstick as your guide, cut the piece in half lengthwise with a utility knife, creating 2 pieces each 1½" wide. Repeat with the second 3"-wide strip, and set aside.

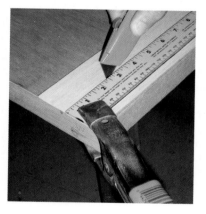

NOTE: Don't use a clamp or vise directly on the soft wood, as it will crush the wood and make dents in the surface.

2. CREATE THE FRAME BOX

2a. Using the same method as before, cut the ³⁄₁₆" strips of balsa in half lengthwise.

2b. From the backside of the frame — glass removed — measure the inside dimensions of the long sides of its lip (where the glass would rest). Saw 2 strips of the split ³⁄₁₆" balsa to the exact length of the long side measurement of the frame lip. Lightly sand their ends to remove any splintering. Stood on its edge, each balsa strip should fit snugly into the long sides of the frame lip.

2c. With the 2 long strips in place, take the measurement of the 2 short sides of the frame lip (the area of clearance between the 2 long balsa strips placed into the frame). Cut 2 pieces of the ³⁄₁₆" balsa to fit inside the 2 long frame box pieces, and sand their ends to remove any splintering. When placed on edge, each of these short pieces should fit snugly inside the long pieces, creating the frame box.

2d. Remove the 2 short pieces and dab their ends with wood glue (use the glue sparingly; balsa wood accepts wood glue remarkably well). Fit the box construction inside the frame to hold its form and let dry.

2e. Remove the 4-sided box construction from the frame and place it on a flat work surface. Place the 11"×14" mirror facedown over the frame box. Miter-cut 4 pieces of 1" corner trim, to case the edge of the mirror and the sides of the frame box. Run wood glue along the inside edge of the corner trim (the side that meets the box). Place the corner trim into position and let dry.

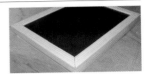

3. PREP THE IMAGES

3a. Since these images were selected to fit within an 11"×14" frame vertically in 1½" sections, each image was sized to 10½" wide. Flip the frame box over, and take the exact measurement of the inside of the box from top to bottom, lengthwise (for this frame box, the measurement was 13⅝"). In a miter box, cut 6 pieces of the 3/32" balsa to the determined length, to fit the inside length of the box snugly without bowing. Lightly sand the ends of each piece to remove any splintering.

3b. With a paper cutter or X-Acto knife, slice each image into 1½" strips, vertically. Start with the image that will be viewed from the left. Working over newspaper, spray the backside of one 1½" image strip, and press onto a 1½" balsa piece.

Repeat with all but the far right section of the image, which is to be spray-mounted and placed into the right interior side of the frame box. (If your image is not 14" long, establish a centered placement on the balsa piece first, mark the wood lightly with a pencil, then use the spray mount and place.)

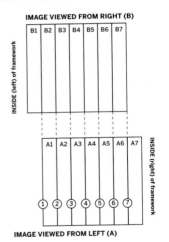

IMAGE VIEWED FROM RIGHT (B)

| B1 | B2 | B3 | B4 | B5 | B6 | B7 |

INSIDE (left) of framework

| A1 | A2 | A3 | A4 | A5 | A6 | A7 |

INSIDE (right) of framework

① ② ③ ④ ⑤ ⑥ ⑦

IMAGE VIEWED FROM LEFT (A)

3c. Using the image placement diagram (at right) as a guide, spray-mount the sections of the image to be viewed from the right on the backsides of the 6 balsa pieces. Image section B2 will be backed with image section A1; B3 backed with A2, etc. The far left section of the image will be placed on the left interior side of the frame box.

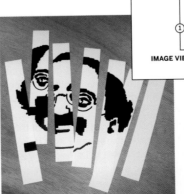

NOTE: To keep from smudging the image or getting spray adhesive on your hands, put a clean sheet of paper over the mounted image, and press it out firmly with your hand.

4. PLACE THE IMAGES

4a. To position the balsa strips within the frame box, first measure and pencil-mark the 1½" points along the top and bottom front edges of the frame box. Next, make vertical guidelines on the inside of the frame box, from the guide marks on its top edge to the bottom where it meets the mirror.

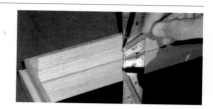

4b. Dab some wood glue along the top and bottom edges of the first balsa section (the one mounted with image sections B2 and A1), and slide it into its frame box position using the pencil markings as your guide. Repeat with the remaining 5 balsa sections. Let dry.

5. ASSEMBLE IT ALL TOGETHER

5a. Completely wipe all fingerprints and dust from the mirror with glass cleaner. Place the frame facedown, and place the glass inside. Place the frame box facedown into the frame. With a miter box, cut 4 pieces of ½" quarter round trim to 6" lengths. Run a thin line of wood glue along both flat sides of the quarter-round trim pieces, and place onto the backside of the frame, pushed firmly against the 4 sides of the frame box. Let dry.

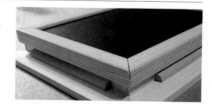

5b. Center a screw eye on each long section of the corner trim, about 2" from the top edge of the frame box, and screw into place. Run picture-hanging wire through the screw eyes and twist securely into place.

FINISH X

The finished Optical Delusion in full effect with Groucho Marx on the left, author Matt Maranian in the middle, and Nina Hagen on the right.

Bagalopes

The bagalope, a simple gift bag made from an envelope, is a project I've shared with countless people over many years. I'm still tickled by their reaction when they learn how it's created. "That bag started as an envelope? No way." Never has the term "pushing the envelope" been truer than with this practical paper project.

You will need: An envelope, glue stick, liquid glue, scissors, ruler, scoring tool, pencil, rubber stamps, ink pads

1. Seal and decorate.

Seal the flap of your envelope down using a glue stick. Be careful not to glue the front to the back or your bag won't open. If you want to decorate the sides of your bag, do so now while it's still flat. I love to rubber-stamp over the surface using various colored inks and stamp images. Let the ink dry thoroughly before you begin the next step, or you'll risk smearing your ink.

2. Score lines and open bag.

Measure and score a line about 1" in from all the edges of the envelope. After scoring, fold back and forth on the lines to "loosen" them up. Trim about ¼" off one of the short ends of the envelope.

3. Shape your bag.

Put your hand in the envelope to open it up. With your hand inside, press down on the short end to flatten it out. The bag will begin to practically shape itself. Push in on the long sides and gently pinch along the fold lines. Just like magic, your bag appears. You should have 2 triangles sticking out of the bottom of the bag. Apply glue to the triangle sides, and press them down so they touch the bag's bottom. Press with your fingers until the triangles adhere completely.

4. Make the final fold and add finishing touches.

After the bottom is secure, all you need to do is fold the top portion of the bag inward to give it a strong lip for attaching optional handles, bows, or other fun embellishments. Too cute!

➕ For details on a fanning option and ideas on how to embellish your bag, check out craftzine.com/05/quick_bagalope.

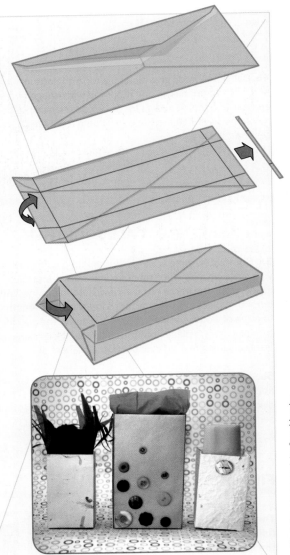

Stephanie Scheetz (coolcrafting.com) has been a designer and instructor in the craft industry for nearly 15 years. Her hobbies include thrift store shopping, eBaying, and collecting mail art, prison art, and bad art.

Illustrations by Tim Lillis; photograph by Sam Murphy

Japanese Stab Binding
Create a personalized hand-bound notebook.

BY CHRISTY PETTERSON

Perhaps because I've always loved writing, bookbinding caught my attention at a really young age. Even when I'm not writing a masterpiece, I love a hand-bound book for doodling, jotting down ideas, and keeping track of things to do.

Japanese stab binding is particularly nice because even though it's easy to produce, the end result looks really complicated, which is good for impressing your mom.

The supplies are basically things you can find around your house, and as long as you aren't going to use the book for something that requires archival considerations, these books are a golden opportunity for recycling. Use old envelopes, brown grocery bags, half-finished notebooks — go nuts!

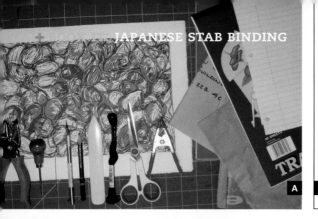

JAPANESE STAB BINDING

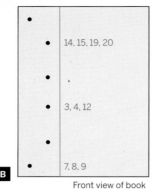

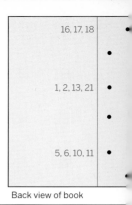

Front view of book   Back view of book

A   B

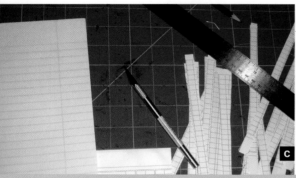

C   D

Fig. A: You probably already have most of the supplies needed for bookbinding. Fig. B: Follow this diagram to keep track of which hole to sew through next.

Fig. C: Using a cutting board with a grid and a cork-back metal ruler will make cutting the paper much easier. Fig. D: Use a clamp to keep the paper from sliding around while creating holes with an awl.

Materials

» **Decorative paper** for the cover
» **Paper (any kind)** for the insides
» **Embroidery thread** or any kind of thread that matches the cover
» **Cutting board** A grid is very helpful for measuring. If you don't have a board, use an old piece of cardboard.
» **Scissors**
» **X-Acto knife or utility knife**
» **Awl or mini hole punch** or the sharp end of a drawing compass
» **Bone folder** or a big popsicle stick
» **Sewing needle** with large eye
» **Ruler** A cork-back metal one is best.
» **Clamp**
» **Pencil**

NOTE: You can adjust the measurements in this project to make any size book you want. You can even customize the size to fit perfectly into your tote or purse.

1. Make your cover.

Pick decorative paper for the cover of the book. Cut 2 pieces of cover paper 5½"×7½". Using your bone folder, fold a flap on each cover that is 1" deep so that the cover now measures 4½"×7½".

2. Create your pages.

Cut a stack of paper 4"×7½" with as many pages as you like. Be creative and pick a variety of different colors, textures, and patterns — paper you might not traditionally see in a book. I chose to cut up notebook paper, tracing paper, an old ledger book, a few brown lunch bags, used manila envelopes, and an old orange and white envelope.

3. Prep and punch your holes.

Draw a template for where your holes will go. The top and bottom holes are ⅜" from the top and bottom edges, and about ⅜" from the left edge. You'll also have 4 holes in the middle; these are ¾" from the spine and about 1¼" apart from each other.

Clamp your cover and inside papers together with the template on top. The clamp might leave a mark on the cover, so it's a good idea to slip a piece of scrap paper between the clamp and cover pages.

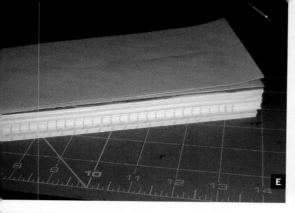

E

F

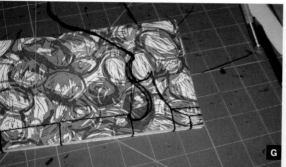
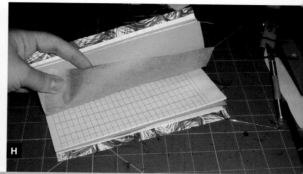

G

H

Fig. E: Use a variety of paper to make the book more interesting. Fig. F: Follow the pattern to stitch the book together.

Fig: G: The stitching is on the outside with stab binding, which adds an extra decorative element. Fig: H: All stitched together, the book is ready for some creative ideas!

Using your awl (or hole punch), create holes that go through the entire stack.

4. Stitch up your book.

Choose thread that matches the cover, and cut it 5 times the length of the spine. Stitching this may seem confusing the first time, but you'll soon see how orderly it is. Starting in the middle, you're both creating a straight line down the side and "wrapping the spine" at several given points.

» Starting on the backside, sew through hole #1, leaving a tail about 4½" long. Wrap the thread around the spine; sew through this hole again (#2).
» Sew through hole #3, wrap the spine, and sew through that hole again (#4).
» Sew through hole #5, wrap the spine, and sew through that hole again (#6).
» Sew through hole #7, wrap the spine, and sew through that hole again (#8).
» Wrap around the bottom edge of the book; sew through that hole again (#9).
» Sew through hole #10, wrap the bottom edge, and go through that hole again (#11).
» Sew through holes #12, #13, and #14. Wrap the

spine and go through the last hole (#15) again.
» Sew through hole #16, wrap the spine, and sew through the same hole (#17).
» Wrap around the top edge of the book and sew through the same hole (#18).
» Sew through hole #19, wrap the top edge of the book, and sew through the same hole (#20).
» Thread the needle with the tail so that both ends of the thread are through the needle.
» Sew through hole #21, but not all the way through the hole, such that the 2 threads end up on the inside of the book (a few pages in).
» Now take the 2 ends, tie them together tightly, and cut them so they are 1"–2" long.

Now that you know the trick to Japanese stab binding, do a little research on more complicated patterns. You can also make up your own patterns. With variations on stitches, color, thread, paper, and texture, your options are limitless!

Christy Petterson is co-editor of getcrafty.com and co-organizer of the Indie Craft Experience in Atlanta. Her line of handmade accessories is called a bardis. abardis.com

The Paper Bag Scrapbook

Refashion lunch sacks to hold memories instead of sandwiches. BY MARCIA FRIEDMAN

The humble brown paper lunch sack has become a bright star in the scrapbooking world. Forget the fancy $8 to $20 store-bought mini albums. Using a few of these familiar bags, a glue stick, some embellishments, and decorative papers, you can create a unique showcase for your photos.

Paper bag scrapbooks have become one of my favorite gift ideas; I've used them for hostess thank yous, bridal and baby shower presents, and family Christmas gifts. There are endless possibilities for page design, and because of the size, they're a snap to assemble. Plus, one end of the page serves as a pocket for memorabilia, journaling cards, or extra photos.

I've used 3 bags to create a 12-page book here, but you can use 2 bags for a smaller 8-page book, or up to 5 bags for a 20-page volume. Twenty pages with decorations and photos become a nice, chunky book, but I wouldn't go any larger than that.

Here are basic instructions for the core of the book and also some sample pages, insert pages, and the covers I created. This is *your* project, with *your* memories, so use these as a guide and get crafty!

Basic Instructions

1. Fold. Using the standard 12"×6" lunch bags, fold each bag in half, so that your pages will be 6"×6". Use a bone folder or the edge of a spoon to make the fold nice and sharp.

2. Arrange. Open the bags flat and lay them one on top of the other, open end to closed end. Then fold the pile in half, and you're ready to decorate each set of pages.

3. Decorate. It's a good idea to work on each 2-page spread in the book form, so you don't accidentally glue the decorative papers to the pages in the wrong order.

4. Bind. When the pages are complete, bind the book by wrapping colored cord, yarn, or ribbon around the inside center of the book; tie it in a knot and a bow along the outer spine. Finish by adding your photos, journaling, and memorabilia.

General Guidelines

» Use a glue stick to adhere the decorative papers to the paper bag pages. Don't worry if the bag shows at the edges; that's part of the charm of this kind of book. Vellum tape (found in craft and scrapbook stores) is best for attaching transparent vellum papers; there's no show-through. Use archival adhesive (there are several types on the market) to adhere your photos to the pages.

» The open end of each bag will become sandwiched between the page and the decorative papers. You'll use the opening to insert pages that you can use for more photos or for journaling. You can also skip these pages and put souvenirs inside.

» Choose colors that work well with your photos and enhance your theme. Because my book is about a winter vacation, I used cool colors throughout.

Each spread requires 2 different papers. Coordinate the papers with colors and patterns that appeal to you. Simple, abstract, muted designs will allow your photos to pop off the page.

» A single 3½"×5" photo works best on this size page, but cropping some pictures smaller will allow you to put 2 or 3 on a page.

Sample Pages

"Let It Snow" Pages

Supplies: **Two 6"×6" squares of printed paper, two 2"×6" strips of cardstock, snowflake stickers, chalk, small alphabet stamps, stamp pad ink**

Glue the squares of printed paper to the first 2 pages of your book. Tear along the long edge of the coordinating cardstock to reveal a rough edge. Use a cotton swab to daub chalk along that rough edge. Glue the strips to the outside edges of each page.

Adhere several snowflake stickers to the cardstock, overlapping the printed paper background in several places. Use the alphabet stamps to create your title at the top of the pages.

Souvenir Pocket Pages

Supplies: **Two 6"×6" squares of printed paper, one 6"×6" square of printed vellum paper, vellum adhesive, 4 large brads, 12" sticker strip, alphabet stamps, stamp pad ink**

Cut the square of printed vellum paper in half along the diagonal. Use the vellum adhesive to glue each resulting triangular piece to a square of the printed paper. Only glue along the side and bottom edges, *not* the long diagonal edge. This will create a pocket

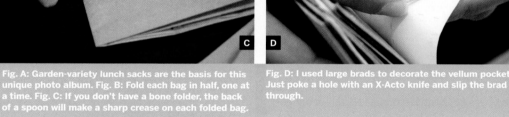

Fig. A: Garden-variety lunch sacks are the basis for this unique photo album. Fig. B: Fold each bag in half, one at a time. Fig. C: If you don't have a bone folder, the back of a spoon will make a sharp crease on each folded bag.

Fig. D: I used large brads to decorate the vellum pockets. Just poke a hole with an X-Acto knife and slip the brad through.

for your memorabilia, such as tickets, notes, cards, etc.

Cut the 12" sticker strip in half and adhere it to the long diagonal edge of the vellum triangle. This creates a decorative edge to your pocket. Put 1 large brad into each of the 2 diagonal corners on each page. Glue the squares to the next 2 pages of your book. Finish by using the alphabet stamps to create your title at the top of the pages.

Sample Insert Page

I made 3 insert pages for my scrapbook. After the insert pages are complete, punch 2 holes along the outside edge of each page. Stagger the sets of holes down along the edges: punch the holes near the top for the first card, in the middle for the second card, and near the bottom of the page for the last card.

In each hole, tie a length of ribbon (double over 3½") that color-coordinates with your papers, as little flags that stick out from the pockets.

"Let It Snow" Insert Page

Supplies: 6"×6" square of printed paper, 2½"×2½" square of cardstock, decorative shaped punch, fine or medium tip marker, alphabet die cuts

Cut the 2½"×2½" square of cardstock in half along the diagonal. Glue the resulting triangle to opposite corners of the 6"×6" square of printed paper. Punch out several decorative shapes in a coordinating color paper and glue to the triangles.

Use the markers to create stitching along the edges of the page. Use the alphabet die cuts to create your title (Figure H). Alphabet stickers will also work.

My Covers

Supplies: Two 5"×6" sheets of printed or solid paper, one 5"×6" sheet of complimentary paper, two 6" lengths of sticker strip or ribbon

Glue the 2 matching 5"×6" sheets of paper to the fore edge (open side) of the front and back covers. Fold the other sheet of paper in half lengthwise, put adhesive along the edges, and lay your folded book, spine first, into the fold. Press firmly around all the edges to make the seal tight.

Glue the ribbons or stickers over the seam where the edges of the 2 different papers meet. Create the title of your book on the front, using any of the lettering techniques described or just your handwriting (Figure G). Bind as described.

E   F

G   H

Fig. E: Slip souvenir tickets, cards, or other memorabilia into the vellum pocket you created. Fig. F: Ribbon and/or yarn wrapped around the center page and tied along the spine is an easy, decorative way to bind your book.

Fig. G: Front cover with finished binding and decoration. The ribbon tabs on the right are part of the pull-out insert pages. Fig. H: The open ends of the lunch-bag pages hold crafty insert pages.

Alternative Ideas

Binding: Close the finished book and drill 3 holes along the spine, about ½" from the edge. Put jump rings (available at office supply stores) through the holes and tie several pieces of ribbon and/or yarn onto each ring.

Be sure to remove the insert cards from each bag before you punch the holes. Also make sure the grommets/brads are a little farther from the inside spine.

Bags: Instead of the plain brown bags, you can use shiny, colored bags as the base. Cut your decorative papers a little smaller than 6"×6" so more of the bags show; this creates a natural page frame that gives another dimension to each spread.

For more sample page how-tos, check out craftzine.com/05/book_paperbag.

At right, details from Marcia's scrapbook.

Marcia Friedman loves letters, inks, and papers. As a professional graphic designer and calligrapher, she gets to indulge these passions full time. She is also an avid photographer.

Cut Paper Mosaic

Make a durable mosaic on the cheap with paper and glue. BY SUSAN BRACKNEY

Maybe it was the wall-to-wall green shag, or the fact that the previous owner had housed 14 cats there, but my charming 1930s bungalow was a steal. The place purportedly had gorgeous hardwood floors throughout, but ripping up the smelly-cat carpeting had revealed one 8'×10' expanse of ugly pine boards — raw, uneven, and studded with rusty nail heads — smack in the middle of my living room. Turns out that leaving such unfinished business was pretty common back then; nice wood is expensive, and most people had area rugs anyway.

Rather than spend a fortune on refinishing or carpeting, I would do as the Romans did. A nod to Pompeii and my precious pooch, this durable "Beware of Dog" mosaic on the cheap is tiled with paper, not marble, and held together with glue, not grout.

Materials

- » **Design sketch**
- » **Ruler and T square**
- » **Pencil**
- » **Tape measure**
- » **Marker or colored pencil**
- » **Painter's tape**
- » **Lightweight poster board, junk mail envelopes, or magazine pages** in black, white, red, gray, and cream
- » **Paper cutter and scissors**
- » **Jars, cigar boxes** or other containers
- » **Latex or acrylic paint**
- » **Chip brush**
- » **Small paintbrushes**
- » **Elmer's glue**
- » **Small bucket or plastic tub**
- » **Dax window glazing** or other filler product that can expand and contract with temperature changes
- » **Putty knife**
- » **Small, handheld vacuum cleaner**
- » **Envirotex Lite pour-on resin finish**
- » **Rubbing alcohol**
- » **Flat-bottomed bucket**
- » **Paint stir sticks and squeegee**
- » **Hair dryer**
- » **Plastic tarp** at least 4mils thick
- » **Wooden screen molding**
- » **Hammer and small handsaw**
- » **Finishing nails**
- » **Wood stain (optional)**
- » **Friends** especially those who owe you big
- » **The patience of Job**

Before You Start

Not much of a dog person? Almost any simple, bold line art will work well for a cut paper mosaic, so find a design you love. And for those with perfectly pristine wood floors? Create a stand-alone mosaic on a large sheet of plywood for wall mounting instead.

The size of your mosaic will dictate the amount of paper and other supplies you'll need. Measure the area's length and width, and then multiply these numbers to obtain your square footage. Now you can collect the right amount of lightweight poster board and other potential tiling materials.

You'll also need to purchase enough Envirotex sealant to complete the job. One 8-ounce package of the two-part, glossy finish coats up to 4 square feet. My 80-square-foot project required 3 gallons of the stuff. One coat of Envirotex equals nearly 50 coats of traditional varnish.

1. Cut and sort your paper.

While you won't need to amass boxes of heavy tiles, you'll need to cut hundreds and hundreds of tiny paper squares. Depending on the size of your paper cutter, you may need to fold your poster board in half to fit under the cutting arm.

1a. Fold your large poster board in half, and place it in the paper cutter with the folded edge closest to you. Make a ¼" or ½" cut, stopping about 1" above the fold. Move the sheet to the right and continue to make a series of long, attached strips.

When you've reached the end of the sheet, rotate the piece (which will look a bit like a clunky grass skirt) so that the fold is to your left. Bring the cutting blade down hard at ¼" or ½" intervals to create multiple tiny squares. Once you get to the end, you'll have just the leftover, folded area. It will be too small to safely cut with the paper cutter, so you may want to use scissors to cut this part into squares.

1b. Because tiles of white and cream paper can look similar, be sure to put these and other colors in separate, labeled containers as you go.

2. Prepare the area.

2a. Use painter's tape to mask off the outer edge of the area to be tiled.

2b. Apply a coat of light-gray latex or acrylic paint over the entire work surface. This color will show between the tiles you place. Let dry completely.

2c. Use a putty knife to apply Dax window glazing to any large cracks or holes in the work surface. Removing any excess as you go, smooth the filler material flush with your floor. Allow 2–3 hours for the glazing to set up (it won't harden completely).

3. Transfer your sketch.

3a. "Squaring up" is one of the easiest ways to transfer

Fig. A: "Squaring up" the sketch makes transferring the image on a large scale easier. Fig. B: The design transfer is complete, and the gluing begins. Fig. C: Spreading Elmer's glue in a small area in order to tile part of the dog's ear. (Meanwhile, Taco the dog carefully supervises.) Fig. D: A little glue on the end of the brush makes picking up and placing individual tiles a snap.

the contents of a small drawing to a larger area. Using a pencil and ruler, draw a grid of 1" squares over the top of your mosaic sketch. If you like, you can use letters across the top and numbers down the left side of the grid for easy reference.

3b. Count the number of boxes on your drawing, and lightly draw with a colored pencil and T square to re-create the same number of boxes on your larger work surface. In my case, eight 1" boxes on my design sketch came out to eight 1' squares on my floor, but the ratio of the size of your sketch to the size of your mosaic area might produce a slightly different scale for you.

3c. Use a pencil to transfer just what you see in grid A-1, A-2, etc., into their corresponding areas on the mosaic surface. If you like, go back over your lines with a marker or a very dark colored pencil.

4. Glue those tiles.

4a. So that you won't need to tread on areas you've already tiled, it's best to work from one end of your design out. (Psst! Grab a pillow to place under your knees, and don't forget to take breaks.) To start tiling,

pour about 1" of Elmer's glue into a small bucket or plastic tub, and use the chip brush to paint a fairly thick coat of glue in one 6" area at a time.

4b. Gather several cut paper squares, dip the tip of a small paintbrush into glue, and then pick up one square at a time by touching the tip of the brush to the middle of the square. With just enough glue, the square magically sticks to the end of your brush!

4c. Stick each square down one at a time onto the glued mosaic surface, making sure to leave equal amounts of space around each. You may find the need for a custom shape or two. Use scissors to cut triangles or skinny rectangles as needed.

NOTE: For a softer look, I mixed cream squares with white squares for the background, and gray squares with black squares for the dog's body. The border areas, however, are tiled solely with black and white for maximum contrast.

4d. In between gluing sessions, cover the mosaic with your tarp to protect your work. Completing my mosaic took several weeks, so be patient!

Fig. E: To soften the look of large expanses of background, mix cream-colored squares with white.
Fig. F: Nail the screen molding into place.

Fig. G: Use the squeegee to pull Envirotex Lite across the unsealed areas. Fig. H: Taco approves of the finished piece.

5. Prepare to seal.

5a. Once all the paper tiles are glued down and the glue has dried completely, use a small, handheld vacuum over the entire work surface to remove any stray hairs or dirt. You may lose some tiles along the way, so replace them as needed.

5b. With the hammer and finishing nails, attach strips of wooden screen molding around the perimeter of your mosaic. Use the small handsaw to cut pieces to fit and to create miter joints at the 4 corners.

5c. Vacuum the entire surface once more to avoid trapping debris under your glossy sealant.

6. Mix and pour sealant.

6a. Thoroughly mix equal parts of Envirotex resin and hardener in your bucket, scraping its sides and bottom frequently with the stir stick. This process shouldn't take more than 2 minutes.

⚠ **WARNING: Avoid contact with eyes or skin, and use only in a very well-ventilated area.**

6b. Pour a uniform coat of sealant in a line along one end of your mosaic. I mixed and poured ½ gallon at a time. Then use a squeegee to uniformly spread the sealant over the top of the mosaic.

6c. You'll see many tiny bubbles trapped under the sealant surface. Run a hair dryer on its hottest setting 1"–2" above the surface to smooth it out.

7. Clean up and wait.

7a. Clean up any stray sealant on your hands or tools with rubbing alcohol.

7b. Allow the mosaic surface coating to cure completely. This can take 3 days to 1 week.

8. Add finishing touches.

Paint or stain the wooden screen molding trim, if you like. Once your mosaic has cured, you may decide you want an even thicker coat. In that case, you can apply a second coat of sealant.

Susan Brackney is an avid crafter, beekeeper, blogger, and author of *The Lost Soul Companion* as well as the sequel, *The Not-So-Lost Soul Companion*. lostsoulcompanion.com

Tin Can Tiles

Tile anything from a small roof to an outdoor bar with some simple can construction. BY MISTER JALOPY

Garage sale proprietors are perplexed when I purchase dusty tin cans from the darkest corners of their abandoned garages. Though my workshop shelves have long been filled with forgotten cans of congealed goo, I find it difficult to resist the crisp design and brash colors of unbridled consumer optimism. At some point I stopped thinking about them as cans, instead considering the cans and printed sheet metal as a raw material. It's no longer a collection of cans, but simply storage and inspiration for future projects.

Would this roof repel the worst that nature could throw at it? Very unlikely. But sheet metal can construction is perfect to roof an outdoor bar, to line the kitchen junk drawer, or reinvent an old steamer trunk.

Photography by Mister Jalopy

Fig. A: The lowly can opener is a remarkably evolved and effective tool in the arsenal. Fig. B: Cans have a soldered seam at the top and bottom that needs to be removed to allow flattening.

Fig. C: Rubbing compound will rub the paint right off, so go slow. Fig. D: Perhaps the most compelling attribute of my low-buck sheet metal brake is that it can be stored in a drawer when not in use. Compact!

Materials

- » Leather gloves
- » Tinsnips
- » Can opener
- » Pointy punch
- » Smooth-faced hammer
- » 18" chunks of 2" angle iron (2)
- » C-clamps (2)
- » Rubbing compound
- » Small brass nails
- » Lots and lots of old cans, metal thermometers, license plates, and Chinese checker boards

 GENERAL SAFETY WARNING

Wear leather gloves. Sheet metal edges are *sharp*, and it's incredibly easy to cut yourself. Do us all a favor and invest in or scrounge up some gloves.

1. Remove unwanted parts of can.

Start by removing the top and bottom with the can opener (Figure A) to create a can tube. Next, removing the entire section of unprinted steel on the side with tinsnips will eliminate the stiff welded seam and leave a flexible piece of metal that can be sweet-talked into being flat.

2. Flatten metal. Be careful!

After removing the bottom and top rims with tinsnips (Figure B), the can will be a reasonably flat and pliable piece of sheet metal that you can unroll. With all the rounded edges cut off, you are left with a 4-sided razor blade of death. The sharp edges will need to be folded in (Step 4 and Figure D) so that they're hidden.

3. Clean and stylize with rubbing compound.

Rubbing compound (available at auto parts stores) has enough grit to remove years of abuse and oxidation (Figure C). This is also a great way to fake patina, as the original printing will be selectively removed where vigorously rubbed.

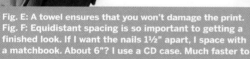

Fig. E: A towel ensures that you won't damage the print. Fig. F: Equidistant spacing is so important to getting a finished look. If I want the nails 1½" apart, I space with a matchbook. About 6"? I use a CD case. Much faster to use whatever is at hand than constant measuring. Fig. G: Cans are so thin that wrapping them around an edge is easy with little hammer taps. Fig. H: Lay the cans out before and you will avoid the mistakes I made.

4. Bend in the sharp edges.

Clamp a couple chunks of angle iron together to create a very cheap, reasonably effective sheet metal brake to bend the sharp edges in. Slip ⅜" of the can edge between the angle iron and tighten the clamps to hold it steadfast. Now you can bend the remaining can to create 90° edges.

If Buddha had a hammer, it would likely be very similar to my darling Proto nickel-plated metal-working hammer. Don't have Buddha's hammer? You will get wonderful results with any smooth-faced hammer. After creating the 90° edge bends in your brake, hammer the bend until it is flat against the metal (Figure D). Repeat for all 4 sides until there are no sharp edges.

❋ **TIP: Hammering on a towel will assure that you don't damage the printed awesomeness of the old can (Figure E).**

5. Pierce holes for nails.

Use a sharp metal punch to pierce holes for the nails (Figure F). For the correct old-timey look, I use tiny, brass, round-head brads to affix the cans to the wood base. Equal distance between the nails will make a huge difference in the aesthetics and polish of the end product.

❋ **TIP: If you nail the can to the backside of the wood, you can fold and coax the can around edges with a little motivation from your hammer (Figure G).**

6. Layer cans.

Like roofing shingles, keep laying cans on top of one another in a reasonably artful way (Figure H).

Mister Jalopy's tin can roof first appeared as part of his Guerrilla Drive-In Theater in MAKE, Volume 11.

Mister Jalopy breaks the unbroken, repairs the irreparable, and explores the mechanical world at hooptyrides.com.

Photograph of MAKE 11 cover by Robyn Twomey

Tropical Fish Scarf

Knit a school of flashy fish to wear around your neck. BY DORA RENEE WILKERSON

This pattern is for the fashionable and whimsical. I was inspired by my daughter, Brianna, who loves fashion and dress-up. She always wants something that the other girls don't have, so I found some fun, colorful yarn and made her this flashy scarf. All her girlfriends want one now.

If you look closely at the pattern, it looks like a little school of fish. You could easily add googly eyes to make the fish stand out more. This is an intermediate-level pattern. The stitch used for this scarf is the flat stitch (similar to the stockinette stitch), which can get tight, so make sure to keep it loose. To learn the flat stitch, visit craftzine.com/go/tropicalfish.

Fig. A: Here are all the pegs wrapped. You only use one row on your board, not both (pretend it's a rake, not a board). Fig. B: Taking the yarn from peg 12 and placing it on peg 11. To decrease, take the bottom yarn from peg 11 and pull up over the top yarn and off the peg. Fig. C: Front view of the last 2 pegs. Fig. D: Knitting off the pegs.

Materials

» **1 skein Red Heart Bright & Lofty yarn** color Jelly Bean
» **1 skein Caron Bliss yarn** color Passion
» **Board loom** Get a small Knifty Knitter; you'll use it as a rake instead of a board.
» **Yarn needle**
» **Crochet hook**
» **Scissors**

1. Cast on.

Cast on your loom, using all 12 pegs. Do only one row on your board, like a rake (Figure A). (This is not a double-knitted item.)

2. Knit your first fish.

» **Rows 1–10:** Flat stitch and knit off (KO).
» **Row 11:** Decrease 1 peg on each side of your loom. Take the yarn from peg 1 and put it on peg 2, KO.

Take the yarn from peg 12 and put it on peg 11, KO (Figure B). Wrap pegs 11–2, KO. (When I say wrap, you are still doing the flat stitch, the only stitch used in this whole pattern.)

» **Row 12:** Decrease 1 peg on each side of the loom. Take the yarn from peg 2 and put it on peg 3, KO. Take the yarn from peg 11 and put it on peg 10, KO. Wrap pegs 3–10, KO.
» **Row 13:** Wrap pegs 10–3 and knit off. Decrease 1 peg on each side of the loom. Take the yarn from peg 3 and put it on peg 4, KO. Take the yarn from peg 10 and put it on peg 9, KO. Wrap pegs 4–9, KO.
» **Row 14:** Wrap pegs 9–4, KO. Decrease 1 peg on each side of the loom. Take the yarn from peg 4 and put it on peg 5, KO. Take the yarn from peg 9 and put it on peg 8, KO. Wrap pegs 5–8, KO.
» **Row 15:** Wrap pegs 8–5, KO. Decrease 1 peg on each side of your loom. Take the yarn from peg 8 and put it on peg 7, KO. Take the yarn from peg 5 and put it on peg 6, KO. Wrap pegs 6 and 7, KO.

This finishes your first fish.

3. Knit additional fish.

» **Row 16:** Increase 1 peg (5). Wrap pegs 5–7, KO.
» **Row 17:** Increase 1 peg (8). Wrap pegs 8–5, KO.

Photography by Dora Renee Wilkerson

» **Row 18:** Increase 1 peg (4). Wrap pegs 4–8, KO.
» **Row 19:** Increase 1 peg (9). Wrap pegs 9–4, KO.
» **Row 20:** Increase 1 peg (3). Wrap pegs 3–9, KO.
» **Row 21:** Increase 1 peg (10). Wrap pegs 10–3, KO.
» **Row 22:** Increase 1 peg (2). Wrap pegs 2–10, KO.
» **Row 23:** Increase 1 peg (11). Wrap pegs 11–2, KO.
» **Row 24:** Increase 1 peg (1). Wrap pegs 1–11, KO.
» **Row 25:** Increase 1 peg (12). Wrap pegs 12–1, KO.
All of your pegs will be full again with yarn.
» **Rows 26–30:** Flat-stitch all your pegs, KO.
» **Row 31:** Decrease one peg on each side of your loom. Take the yarn from peg 1 and put on peg 2, KO. Take the yarn from peg 12 and put on peg 11, KO. Wrap pegs 11–2, KO.
» **Row 32:** Wrap pegs 2–11, KO. Decrease 1 peg on each side of your loom. Take the yarn from peg 2 and put it on peg 3, KO. Take the yarn from peg 11 and put it on peg 10, KO. Wrap pegs 3–10, KO.
» **Row 33:** Wrap pegs 10–3, KO. Decrease 1 peg on each side of your loom. Take the yarn from peg 3 and put it on peg 4, KO. Take the yarn from peg 10 and put it on peg 9, KO. Wrap pegs 4-9, KO.
» **Row 34:** Wrap pegs 9–4, KO. Decrease 1 peg on each side of your loom. Take the yarn from peg 4 and put it on peg 5, KO. Take the yarn from peg 9 and put it on peg 8, KO. Wrap pegs 5–8, KO.
» **Row 35:** Wrap pegs 8–5, KO. Decrease one peg on each side of your loom. Take the yarn from peg 8 and put it on peg 7, KO. Take the yarn from peg 5 and put on peg 6, KO. Wrap pegs 6–7, KO.

You just finished your second fish! For each additional fish, repeat rows 16–35. Keep going until you've reached your desired length. I did this scarf for a total of 15 fish.

4. Knit your last fish.

Your first and last fish are larger than the rest.
To knit your last fish:
» **Row 36:** Increase 1 peg (5). Wrap pegs 5–7, KO.
» **Row 37:** Increase 1 peg (8). Wrap pegs 8–5, KO.
» **Row 38:** Increase 1 peg (4). Wrap pegs 4–8, KO.
» **Row 39:** Increase 1 peg (9). Wrap pegs 9–4, KO.
» **Row 40:** Increase 1 peg (3). Wrap pegs 3–9, KO.
» **Row 41:** Increase 1 peg (10). Wrap pegs 10–3, KO.
» **Row 42:** Increase 1 peg (2). Wrap pegs 2–10, KO.
» **Row 43:** Increase 1 peg (11). Wrap pegs 11–2, KO.
» **Row 44:** Increase 1 peg (1). Wrap pegs 1–11, KO.
» **Row 45:** Increase 1 peg (12). Wrap pegs 12–1, KO.
» **Rows 46–56:** Flat-stitch all pegs and KO.

5. Crochet off the loom.

Take your scarf completely off the loom with a crochet hook by doing a chain stitch. Add a knot to secure it, and weave in any ends that may be left over.

6. Add the fringe.

Now it's time to add your fringe. Take yarn from both your Red Heart and your Caron Bliss skeins, and cut it into 4" lengths. Add these to your fish (Figure E), but do not add them where your work folds in (you want to show that). I like to add the Caron Bliss on both sides first because it brings out the contrasting colors. Then wear it — see Briana Wilkerson modeling the final product below. Super cute!

E

F

Dora Renee Wilkerson lives in Marion, Ohio, with her husband and two children. They have a small farm where they raise many animals. bricoreandfamily.blogspot.com

Easy House Slippers

Do as the Norwegians do and make these super-simple slippers. BY LIECEL TVERLI SCULLY

There's a saying where I'm from: "Don't just sit there with your hands in your lap — knit something!" I grew up in the far north of Norway, above the Arctic Circle in Saltdal, a small town on the edge of a fjord. Knitting was the perfect way to pass the time during the dark, cold winters. At school, knitting class was a requirement; when I was in the 5th grade, we had to make a pair of socks using five needles. It was a complicated project, and I remember having a really hard time with it. But my poor friend Roger was so frustrated he threw his half-done sock into the fireplace at home, needles and all!

This is a pattern that's really popular in my valley right now. It's an easy project that makes a fun, cozy slipper. If you know basic knitting, you'll knit these in no time.

Photography by Liecel Tverli Scully

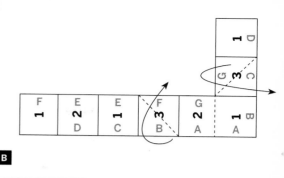

A

B

C

D

Fig. A: The finished knit shape. Fig. B: Diagram for folding and sewing the slipper. Fig. C: Sewing the slipper.

Fig. D: The slippers before felting, a top view (left) and a flattened side view (right).

Materials

» U.S. size 9 knitting needles
» Wool yarn in 3 different colors
  I used PT2 yarn from Norway, but you can use any wool yarn that will felt.

Pattern adjustments for shoe sizes (U.S.)
Size 9 — 20 stitches, 20 rows
Size 8 — 19 stitches, 19 rows
Size 5 — 16 stitches, 16 rows

1. Knit the slipper.
With color 1, cast on 20 stitches, and work garter stitch until your square counts 20 rows (40 times back and forth). Switch to color 2 and repeat, following the diagram. When finished with the sixth square, bind off and pick up 20 stitches on the side of that square. Knit the last 2 squares and bind off. You should end up with 8 squares in an L shape (Figure A). Always lift off the first stitch; it leaves a nicer edge.

✱ TIP: Copy and cut out the diagram; try folding in paper before trying to fold the knit project.

2. Fold and sew the slipper.
By folding the knit squares the right way, you'll end up with a slipper! Following the diagram (Figure B), fold along the dotted lines on the long branch of the L and sew points A, B, C, and D together (Figure C). Then fold along the last remaining dotted line and sew points E, F, and G together. The heel will curve around to accommodate, and there will be flaps to lie flat at the ankle like a collar (Figure D). Repeat instructions for a second slipper.

3. Felt the slippers.
The slippers will look big, but don't worry, they will shrink. Throw them in your washing machine and wash them on hot. If they still look big and are not felted enough, wash them again.

Liecel Tverli Scully is an aspiring printmaker who lives in San Francisco with her knitting needles, yarn, and husband. She may be the most northern-born Giants fan (pending review).
luckytravelsinc.blogspot.com

Crochet Caps a la Carte

Build your own hat with this mix-and-match menu.

BY AMY O'NEILL HOUCK

When my grandmother taught me to crochet at the age of 8, she first showed me how to make hats. While I occasionally crocheted other things, over the next 20 years or so I mostly made hats — often silly ones. With so many design possibilities, I never get tired of them.

Each crochet stitch is complete and stands on its own, not dependent on its neighbors; therefore, crochet offers the freedom and stability to create fabric that easily takes any form or shape. Hats are perfect executions of crochet's sculptural qualities. With so many fun ways to mix and match, this tutorial approaches the hat in a build-your-own-sundae menu style.

Photograph by Sam Murphy

Materials

» **Yarn** Any kind will do. One skein makes most baby hats, and 2 skeins most adult hats, but the amount depends on yardage and hook size. Hats are great stash-busters — you can mix and match colors and textures to create a unique piece.

» **Crochet hook** sized to match the yarn you've chosen

» **Scissors**

» **Yarn needle**

» **Trimmings (optional)** such as ribbon, buttons, and such

» **Crochet stitch dictionary (optional)** for inspiration

A

B

1. Pick your fiber and your hook.

All of the hats featured here start at the crown, or top of the head. Crocheting your hats from the crown down means you don't necessarily need to know your gauge (number of stitches per inch) before you begin your project, but you'll want to experiment with your chosen yarn, trying various hook sizes, until you've created a fabric that has the right look and feel for your hat.

❋ **TIP: Practice a new style of hat in baby size (Figure A). You'll get to experiment in small scale and have a hip gift in no time.**

2. Pick a stitch for the hat crown.

Hats are often worked in single crochet because it produces a solid fabric without being too thick. If you want some ventilation to keep cool, consider a more open fabric for the crown, as in this hat by designer Vashti Braha (Figure B).

I often make baby hats in half-double crochet because it's fast, but I still like the way solid single crochet looks — chunky and cute.

3. Start your circle.

To create a hat with a nice, tight center, use an adjustable ring:

a. Wrap the yarn twice around your fingers.

b. Pinch the ring and the tail to hold the ring together.

✂ TO JOIN OR TO SPIRAL?

Whenever you crochet in the round, you can choose to join each round with a slip stitch and use a turning chain to move to the next round, or simply spiral onward, stitching directly from the last stitch of the previous round into the first stitch of the next one. I always work my hats in a spiral to avoid the obvious seam created by joining.

---

c. Insert the hook into the center of the ring and pull up a loop; slip stitch to secure (Figure C).

d. Work 8 stitches into the ring, and join the first stitch to the last with a slip stitch (Figure D).

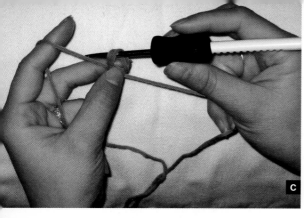
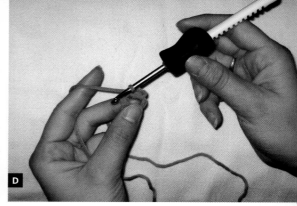

Figs. C, D, and E: Making an adjustable ring to begin crocheting in the round.

Fig. F: Work your increases in 2 ways: staggered (left) or stacked (right).

e. Pull gently on the tail of your ring to close the center. This center might loosen as you work but will stay closed once you weave in your ends (Figure E).

NOTE: Why 8 stitches? Actually, there's no "right" number, and many people start their rings with 6 stitches. Any fewer would probably not make a very round beginning. You could also have more than 8, but too many more would make your hat begin to ruffle and not lay flat.

4. Pick a crown style.

When crocheting the crown, you need to increase at a regular rate to create a flat, round piece of fabric. If you add stitches too quickly, you'll get ruffled fabric, and if you don't add enough, your fabric will curl.

If you start out with 8 stitches in your ring, you'll add 8 stitches per round of the crown of your hat. If you're starting with 6, add 6, and so on. How you add them determines the look of the crown.

If you "stack" your increases by taking care to place each subsequent round of increases in the center of the increase from the previous round, you'll end up with a polygon and an obvious "pinwheel" of increases at the top of the hat.

The polygon shape will give way to a round hat once you start working the sides. In my pageboy cap, I emphasized the polygon shaping with stacked decreases on the underside of the hat (opener). If you want a more rounded crown, just stagger the increases so that you place them either before or after the increase from the row below (Figure F).

5. Pick a crown size.

Work in rounds, increasing regularly until the crown is the size you need for your hat.

a. For a close fit, like a skullcap or a cloche, you'll want to stop increasing when the crown is about 1" shy of the diameter of the top of your head.

b. For a pillbox, fedora, or any average-fitting hat, make the crown exactly the same diameter as the top of your head.

c. For an oversized crown, as in a beret, pageboy, or Rasta cap, just keep increasing until the crown is the size you want — the fit is determined at the brim.

✳ TIP: **You can find a chart of standard head sizes by visiting the Craft Yarn Council of America's website: yarnstandards.com/headsize.html.**

Photography (step-by-step) by James P. Houck

6. Pick a turning style.

When the crown of your hat is the size you need, you can begin crocheting the sides of the hat simply by continuing onward without increases. You'll get a smooth, seamless transition.

If you want to create a deliberate edge between the crown and the sides of the hat, as in the hats in Figures B and I, work the first non-increase round in the back loop only of the stitches in that round, creating a clear fold or crease. Work all subsequent rounds normally.

7. Pick side details.

If you're making a straight-sided hat, the sides are the most visible part and make a great canvas for crochet explorations. Try out a new stitch or color combination (Figure H). To make the ripples, I worked a repeating pattern (sc, hdc, dc, dc, hdc, sc) for one round, then a plain, single crochet round after that. I changed colors every 2 rounds.

Since a hat is nice and small, it's easy to take risks and experiment — don't be afraid to drag out a stitch dictionary or try out a pattern stitch you saw in another project. Give yourself 4 or 5 rounds to see if you like it, and try something else if you don't.

Continue to crochet the hat sides until you've got a length you like. If you're making a tam, beret, or any hat that has an oversized crown, you'll want to decrease after the turn to get the hat back to "head size." You can work a few rounds even, without increases or decreases; if you want a full look, like a Rasta cap, you can begin your decreases immediately after the turning row.

Once the hat is back to head size, work a few rounds without any increases or decreases to create the band that will hold the hat on your head.

8. Pick a brim.

a. If you're making a hat without a brim, you're done. Just weave in your ends.

b. For a classic hat with a rolled or folded brim, work the hat longer than you'd like it to be on your head, then roll it up or fold it into place. You may want to tack the folds up if they won't stay on their own.

c. To add a partial brim as I did in the pageboy cap (opener), you'll work back and forth over 40% of the stitches on the cap. To get the brim to be stiffer than the hat, I doubled the yarn and went down a hook size. Increase at each edge of the brim in the first row, and then decrease at each

G

H

I

Photography by Sam Murphy (G, H) and John H. O'Neill (I)

Smoothing the "bump" when finishing a project in the round. **Fig. L:** Remove the hook and cut the yarn, leaving at least a 6" tail. **Fig. M:** Pull on the tail to undo the last loop that remains after you remove the hook.

Fig. N: Thread the tail onto a yarn needle and insert the needle under and through the V of the next stitch. **Fig. O:** Then insert the hook through the V of the last stitch and tug gently to secure. Weave in the ends.

edge for every subsequent row until the brim is the size you'd like. If the brim gets too small too quickly, make your decreases every other row. Finish by working a row of single crochet around the hat and the brim.

d. To add an all-over brim, you'll want to start increasing again just like you did for the crown — change to a smaller hook to make the brim hold its shape. For a bowler, with a curl at the edge of the brim, stop increasing when the brim is the right size and work a few more rows even to get a nice curl.

✳ TIP: Ear flaps are just like partial brims, but worked over a smaller part of the hat edge, and without changing hook size.

9. Pick your toppings.

You may want to embellish your hat. Here are a couple of ideas.

a. To add a flower:
Chain 2. Six single crochet (sc) in 2nd chain from hook; join with a slip stitch to form a round. Chain 6. Skip next sc and sc in following stitch, to make the first petal. *Chain 6, skip 1 sc, sc in next stitch, repeat from * to make 6 petals total. Chain 4. sc in chain space. *Chain 4, sc in chain space. Repeat from * to make 6 petals total. Fasten off leaving at least 4" tails. Pull all tails to the back of the flower, and attach to the hat.

b. To weave a ribbon through the hat:
Create an eyelet round to make holes for your ribbon. *(Dc into next of the round, ch 1, sk 1 st), repeat from * around (Figure G).

10. Smooth out the bumps.

When you create spiraled rounds, you'll always have a "bump" at the end where one round ends and the other begins. Here's how to hide it.

First remove the hook and cut the yarn. Pull on the tail to undo the last loop that remains. Then thread the tail onto a yarn needle and insert the needle under and through the V of the next stitch. Insert the hook through the V of the last stitch of the round and tug gently to secure. Weave in the ends.

Amy O'Neill Houck crochets, knits, and writes at her home in Washington, D.C., where you'll rarely find her out without a hat. Amy blogs at hookandi.blogspot.com.

Hardware Handbag

Knit a vinyl and metal purse using your favorite toolbox trinkets. BY SALLY L. CONVERSE-DOUCETTE

M y youth was spent in a house constantly "under construction." Although my mother bemoaned the inconvenience, I thought it was a great adventure and loved the doodads left around after projects were complete. Bits of wood, nails, washers, bolts, and beautiful shining metal pieces filled small, neat boxes in our garage, and I helped myself to them liberally.

Also during this time, I developed a love for textiles: wearing them, altering them, knitting, sewing, crocheting, and so on. It's not surprising that I began to combine the two interests, and both still influence my art. My metal knitted purse is an excellent example of textile and hardware fusion.

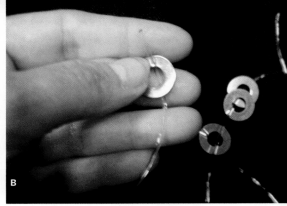

Fig. A: Assorted washers. Fig. B: Stringing the washers onto the vinyl yarn. Remember that the last embellishment added is first knit. Fig. C: Treat with Armor All wipes. It's important to use metal knitting needles and to coat them with Armor All or a similar product from time to time. This will keep vinyl yarn moving smoothly over the needles. Fig. D: Bringing the yarn forward in preparation for knitting an embellishment in place.

Materials

- » **U.S. size 5 metal knitting needles** 24" circular
- » **Yarn** I used 2 skeins of Jelly Yarn fine gauge vinyl yarn, color Ice, found in high-end yarn stores or online at jellyyarns.com.
- » **8" mending braces, zinc (2)**
- » **Assorted washers, wing nuts, grommets, hex and square nuts**
- » **Vinyl protectant** such as Armor All Protectant Wipes or similar product
- » **Craft scissors**
- » **Large-eyed metal needle** for sewing sides and handles of purse and weaving in ends

The materials used in my Hardware Handbag come from a hardware store just a few blocks from my home, but interesting pieces for your bag can be found at larger home improvement stores as well.

Choose embellishments that have holes through the centers large enough to thread the yarn, and make sure they're lightweight so they don't pull your bag out of shape or become too heavy to carry.

In my purse, I use an assortment of stainless steel, nylon, brass, hardened steel, and rubber washers, as well as wing nuts, grommets, and hex and square nuts.

These materials may discolor over time, but they're very unlikely to rust. You will also need two 8" mending braces (zinc) for the purse handles.

Important Things to Know Before Starting Your Bag

» Before casting on, thread all embellishments onto the yarn in reverse order; the last item on will be the first knit.

» This bag is knit using garter stitch. Choose one side to be the front, and place embellishments only on this side. When you arrive at a stitch where you'd like to knit one in, bring the yarn forward, slide a bead down to the needle, slip the next stitch purl-wise, and bring the yarn to the back of the bag.

Fig. E: A recently knit washer. The yarn is now at the back, ready to knit the next normal stitch. **Fig. F:** Sewing in the handles. A large-eyed sewing needle will help.

Fig. G: Sewing the sides of the bag; weave in loose ends. **Fig. H:** The finished bag. Reinforce any particularly heavy embellishments by weaving around them.

» Add your washers, gaskets, and other items to this basic pattern as you desire. Use a graph of the purse's front and back to help you plot out your embellishments ahead of time. An easy way to make a knitting graph is to create a Microsoft Excel spreadsheet with cells that are set with a height of 12.75 points (.45 cm) and width of 3.14 points (.95 cm). A graph of the basic purse pattern would be 40 stitches wide × 171 rows long. It's best not to bead or embellish the handles.

Basic Pattern

» **Gauge:** 4 stitches per inch
» Cast on 40 stitches.
» **Rows 1–22:** Knit each row.
» **Row 23:** Knit first 10 stitches, bind off center 20 stitches, and knit remaining 10 stitches.
» **Rows 24–27:** Knit the first set of 10 stitches back and forth for 4 rows. Cut the yarn, leaving a 15" tail. Join yarn at outer edge of purse and knit 10 stitches on the other side of the purse for 4 rows.
» **Row 28:** Knit first 10 stitches, cast on 20 stitches. Being careful not to twist the stitches you just cast on, join to remaining 10 stitches and knit to end.

» **Rows: 29–141:** Continue knitting every row, placing your embellishments as desired.
» **Row 142:** Repeat instructions for Row 23.
» **Rows 143–146:** Repeat instructions for Rows 24–27.
» **Row 147:** Repeat instructions for Row 28.
» **Rows 148–171:** Knit each row.
» Bind off all stitches.

Finishing

Fold the first 23 rows of the purse toward the back of the purse, encasing one of the mending braces. Using vinyl yarn and a large-eyed sewing needle, stitch around the brace. Repeat this procedure at the other end of the purse. Fold the bag in half and stitch from the bottom of the purse up 4" on both sides of the bag. Weave in any yarn ends.

Don't cut the yarn ends too short as they may work their way out. If you've used any extra-heavy pieces for your embellishments, reinforce them by weaving additional yarn around them. Enjoy.

Sally Converse-Doucette has a BFA in fine arts and theater design, and owns her own graphic design company, slixgrfx. In her spare time she plucks away on her electric guitar.

Woven Memory Basket

Weave your vacation road maps into an attractive souvenir. BY JANE PATRICK

Think of basketry as three-dimensional weaving. If you ever wove paper as a child, that's the basis for this plaited basket. You begin by weaving a flat base, and then upturn the strips (called stakes or weavers) to make the sides, in what is referred to as bias plaiting. You'll be surprised by how sturdy your paper basket will be.

Baskets can be called a true handcraft because almost any basket you'll see anywhere in the world has been woven by hand. It's one craft they just haven't learned to make well by machine.

This project repurposes maps from your travels to weave a practical, attractive basket full of memories of trips taken and experiences had along the way.

A B

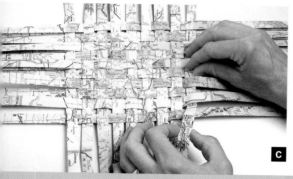

C D

Fig. A: Prepare strips for weaving. With the map turned lengthwise, cut 20 weavers 2" wide. Fig. B: Fold each strip in half lengthwise. Then fold the edges to the center, and finally, fold these edges together, creasing tightly. Fig. C: Weave the base with an over, under, over, under weave. Fig. D: Mark the base by twining around the edges.

Materials

» 2–3 large road maps
» Contrasting string or thread
» Clothespins
» Cutting mat
» Rotary cutter
» Awl or tapestry needle
» Scissors
» Small tweezers
» White glue (optional) to further stiffen the basket

1. Prepare the strips (Figure A). Cut off any parts of the map you don't want to use. With the map turned lengthwise, cut 20 weavers 2" wide (the longer the strips, the larger your basket can be). I made my weavers 37" long, based on the longest length of the map. Fold each strip in half lengthwise (Figure B). Then fold the edges to the center, and finally, fold these edges together, creasing tightly. The more uniform and crisp you make the strips, the better your basket will be.

2. Weave over, under, over, under (plain weave) for a square base, 10 weavers in both directions (Figure C). If you point the folds toward the center of each side, you'll have a better result when you weave the corners.

3. Using string or thread, mark the base by twining around the edges (Figure D). Measure a length of lightweight string 10 times the circumference of the base and fold it in half. Fold this string around a weaver so that one end of the string is underneath the weaver and the other end is on top. To twine, simply twist the ends together between the weavers, then place the top end underneath the next weaver while leaving the bottom end on top. Repeat until you reach the beginning, and tie the ends together.

4. Weave the sides, working one side at a time. Divide the weavers on one side in half and weave the halves together. Beginning with the center weavers, cross them, and weave both out to the edge (Figure E). Weave the remaining weavers in the same manner. Tighten the weavers by pulling out the slack. The weaving will poke out where the weavers cross. This is as it should be, and will be the new corner. You've

Photography by Jane Patrick

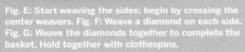

Fig. E: Start weaving the sides; begin by crossing the center weavers. Fig. F: Weave a diamond on each side. Fig. G: Weave the diamonds together to complete the basket. Hold together with clothespins.

Fig. H: Finish the edge by folding weavers over one another and down into the inside. Fig. I: Trim the weavers on the inside of the basket.

now woven a diamond (Figure F). Secure this side with a clothespin. Repeat for the other 3 sides.

5. Join the diamonds by weaving them together. Continue weaving until your basket is as tall as you like it, or until you run out of weaving material (Figure G). You'll notice that if you follow one weaver, it travels from one side of the basket to the other.

6. Finish the edge. Working in pairs, fold one weaver over the other and down into the weaving on the inside, then repeat for the other weaver. Do likewise with all the weavers (Figure H).

7. If you have holes in the bottom or sides of your basket, this means it's not tightly woven. You can fix this by pulling the weavers from the bottom of the basket to the top, to take up the slack. Keep tightening weavers until they are snug against each other.

This is well worth the effort in the final product. Once you're satisfied with the tightness of the weave, check the top edge to see that it's even and then trim the ends on the inside (Figure I).

8. To create a flat, sturdy base, I place the basket over a container and then weight the bottom with something heavy, like a rock.

After a few hours, I crease along the bottom edges for a basket that sits flat and stable on the table. If you want a very stiff basket, you can dilute white craft glue with water and paint the basket inside and out.

Variation: Newspaper Baskets
The Sunday funny papers are a colorful choice for basket weaving. I choose the funnies with the brightest colors. A monochromatic alternative is a basket woven of pages devoid of photos with lots of small print, such as want ads. After weaving, I treat the surface with melted beeswax for a muted, aged appearance.

Jane Patrick is vice president of sales for loom and spinning wheel manufacturer Schacht Spindle Co., Inc., and the author of *Time to Weave: Simply Elegant Projects to Make in Almost No Time* (Interweave Press). She lives in Boulder, Colo.

Treasure Box

Build and embellish a vintage-style box to store precious jewels. BY SUSAN BEAL

I f you love jewelry, why not make a pretty, vintage-inspired box to house your treasures? The sparkly floral rhinestone design echoes Enid Collins' embellished handbags of the 1960s, while the colors, trim, and details are ultra-customizable to suit your own taste.

A row of hooks on the inside lid is perfect for necklaces and earrings, while bracelets, rings, and brooches sit neatly on an interior tray that lifts right out. The velvet-lined bottom of the box is perfect for larger pieces or longer necklaces. This is a lightweight box designed for storage, but not a lot of heavy use, so be sure to handle it gently, like any vintage piece!

Materials

- » **¼" birch panels** cut to size: two 9"×10" pieces, two 4"×7½" pieces, two 4"×9", two 8½"×1", and two 7"×1"
- » **Carpenter's glue**
- » **Elastic** 2yds, ¼"- to ½"-wide
- » **Pencil**
- » **Measuring tape or ruler**
- » **Paintbrushes**
- » **Acrylic paint in desired colors** I used Plaid Folk Art Ocean Cruise 2225, Metallic Blue Pearl 670, and Metallic Pure Gold 660.
- » **Bond 527 cement**
- » **Glass pebbles (4)**
- » **Small hooks (6)**
- » **Scissors**
- » **Seam ripper or small awl**
- » **Jewelry or ring tray** 8½"×7½"
- » **Velvet jewelry pads (2)** 7"×7½"
- » **Craft glue** I like Aleene's Tacky Glue.
- » **Cotton swabs**
- » **Small hinges (2, optional)**
- » **¼" gold metallic trim** about 5½yds
- » **⅛" blue satin ribbon** about 2½yds
- » **Assorted rhinestones** I used 5 gold rounds, 31 clear teardrops in varying sizes, and 18 small green marquise shapes.

Build the Box

1. To construct the box, start by attaching the sides to each other, 2 at a time. Using a wall or other 90° angle to prop against, arrange one of your 4"×7½" pieces horizontally, and one of your 4"×9" sides vertically, lining up the sides so they form a perfect L-shaped right angle where they meet (Figure A). Attach them with carpenter's glue, wiping away any excess with a cotton swab. Brace them with a heavy book or weight so that they stay aligned and straight. Let the glue dry until it is set. Repeat for the other 2 sides.

2. Attach the narrow 7"×1" and 8½"×1" pieces of wood to the inside of the angled corners, flush with the bottom. These will form a 1"-tall shelf at the bottom of the box. Glue them down securely with carpenter's glue and let them dry.

3. When both of the wall sets are completely dry, glue them together to form the 4-sided walls of the box. Place them together as shown in Figure B so that the edges join neatly, and attach them with carpenter's glue. Brace them with 2 knotted strands of elastic so that they're held together correctly, and let them dry completely.

4. Take the two 9"×10" panels, which will be the top (lid) and bottom of the box. Place the walls on the bottom panel so they're centered. It's easier to make pencil marks around the perimeter to show where the box walls will go. Remember that the shelf will be on the lower section of the walls.

5. Apply carpenter's glue, following your pencil marks, on the box bottom, and firmly press the 4 glued sides down over it so that the front side is flush with the bottom. Clean up any excess glue with a cotton swab. Let dry completely. Remove the elastic after the box is securely glued in place.

Paint the Box

6. Paint the box and the lid with acrylic paint (Figure C). I chose to make mine blue on the outside and gold on the inside and bottom. I mixed equal parts of 2 shades of blue (Metallic Blue Pearl and Ocean Cruise) to get a brighter, lighter color.

NOTE: If you choose to add hinges, it may be easier if you leave the hinge area unpainted. Just mark off the hinge placement with pencil and paint around that area.

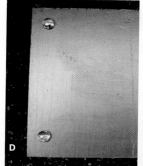

Fig. A: Build the walls. Fig. B: Glue the box together and brace it with elastic. Fig. C: The inside and outside of the box after 3 coats of paint.

Fig. D: Attach "feet" to the bottom. Fig. E: Decorate by adding edging to the box with ribbons and trim.

7. Paint each part of the box, letting each coat dry completely before applying the next. Three coats give a nice, even finish.

8. Meanwhile, paint the edges, sides, and bottom of the jewelry tray (I used gold) to cover the original color. Two or three coats of paint should be perfect.

Make It Fancy

9. Flip the painted box over and use 527 cement to attach the 4 glass pebbles at each corner of the bottom panel. Let dry completely (Figure D).

10. Add trim and ribbon in stages to cover the raw edges and fancy up the box (Figure E). Join each strand on the back of the box, where it isn't as visibly noticeable.

First, use 527 cement to add metallic trim all around the perimeter of the box lid and bottom, overlapping at the back, as well as 2 strips on the top and bottom of the interior lid. Glue metallic trim on the top edges of the jewelry tray as shown.

Now cut two 2½" pieces of ribbon, double each one with the raw ends together, and slip the ends of each loop into the center on both sides of the tray.

Finally, secure with a drop of glue.

You can also glue strands of ribbon around the upper and lower edges of the box sides. Then glue trim on the body of the box, outlining the raw edges of the sides and covering the top edges of the box.

11. Use 527 cement to glue the 2 velvet jewelry pads down, one on the bottom of the box, the other inside the top lid. When they're completely dry, arrange your 6 hooks across the pad on the inside of the lid, spaced evenly. Use your seam ripper or awl to make small holes in the velvet pad so that you can twist each hook into the pad. Add a drop of glue as you screw in each hook to reinforce it (Figure G).

Embellish with Flowers

12. Place the lid on the box to plan your flower design, then use a ruler or measuring tape to plot out rhinestone placement.

13. Use craft glue to attach the first and largest round rhinestone in the exact center of the lid. Now mark the center of each side and measure 1½" in from each mark. Place the 4 smaller round rhinestones here and glue them down (Figure I).

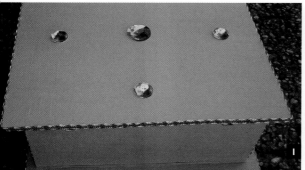
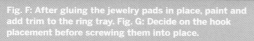

Fig. F: After gluing the jewelry pads in place, paint and add trim to the ring tray. Fig. G: Decide on the hook placement before screwing them into place.

Fig. H: The ring tray nestled inside the finished box.
Fig. I: The center rhinestones glued in place.
Fig. J: The finished daisies and leaves.

14. Arrange the clear teardrop flower petals around each center — 7 for the larger center one and 6 around each smaller one. Glue them down with craft glue (Figure J).

15. Last, you'll add the tiny green leaves by placing marquise-shaped green rhinestones in pairs to complement each flower (Figure J).

Add 4 more pairs at each corner of the design as shown, and glue them down with craft glue. Use a cotton swab to wipe away excess glue. Let them dry completely.

❋ **TIPS: For a sturdier box, use small nails or screws in addition to gluing it together. Don't use 527 cement to attach the rhinestones — it will affect the color and dissolve some of the metallic backing, leaving the stones cloudy. This cement can also damage the paint coating on the box, so be careful as you use it.**

Add Optional Hinges

After Step 9, glue the small hinges to the box lid using 527 cement. Attach the other half of the hinges to the back wall of the box, pressing down firmly. Let dry completely. Be sure not to get any glue in the hinges themselves. Later, you can add trim and ribbon (if desired) to cover the hinge edges.

Jewelry Credits
Daisy brooches: *vintage*
Green brooch: *Cathy of California*
All other jewelry: *Susan Beal*

Material Sources
Glues, rhinestones, paint, brushes: michaels.com
Trim, specialty rhinestones: bergerbeads.net
Jewelry tray and pads: *New Box Corporation,*
 (213) 623-3800 or Rio Grande, riogrande.com

Susan Beal is a Portland writer and designer. She co-wrote *Super Crafty: Over 75 Amazing How-to Projects,* and her jewelry, skirt kits, and writing can be found at susanstars.com and westcoastcrafty.com.

Head Case

Regardless of how many hats and pairs of sunglasses I own, I always find myself wearing the same two favorites. And as far as sunglasses go, at this point in my life I'm done with the $10 carwash variety, so when I park them after a long, sunny day out, I don't want them resting lens-side down getting all scratched up. This hat head serves double duty as a practical place to rest your favorites, while serving as an objet d'art in the off time.

You will need: Plaster of Paris, wire whisk, cheap plastic drip tray for potted plants (8" size), styrofoam wig head, papier-mâché (wood glue, flour, water), exotic foreign newspaper, hot glue, clear "factory finish" spray shellac

1. Pour.

Combine 1 part plaster of Paris to 1 part water, mixing with a wire whisk to remove clumps. Pour to the rim of the drip tray. Let dry.

2. Mâché.

Cut the newspaper into small strips. In a mixing bowl, mix up 1 cup of warm water, ½ cup flour, and 2–3 long squirts of wood glue until smooth. Dip newspaper strips and apply to the styrofoam head, using little pieces around the eyes, nose, ears, and mouth. Let dry.

3. Mount.

Use hot glue to center the head on the upturned plaster base. Mâché over the bottom edge of the neck and down over the plaster base. Tuck the mâché under the bottom edge of the base to create a nice finish (it's good to stand the base on top of a wide roll of masking tape while working, and to let the mâché dry).

4. Adorn.

But maybe it looks so good without, you might just want to keep it that way. At the very least, give it a spray with the shellac finish. Is this where I make some remark about two heads being better than one?

Matt Maranian is a designer and best-selling author who lives in Brattleboro, Vt.

PAPERMAKING

By François Vigneault

Recycle your unwanted bills and junk mail into custom-made personal stationery.

Paper, first invented in China around the 1st or 2nd century A.D., is now so ubiquitous that it has achieved near-invisibility in our modern world. The average American household receives more than 100 pounds of unwanted junk mail each year! However, creating a handmade sheet of paper can remind anyone of this everyday object's noble origins.

Here's a chance to give your unwanted papers a second life for stationery, collage, or anything else you can imagine. Rediscover this ancient and oh-so-easy art form. »

BASICS »

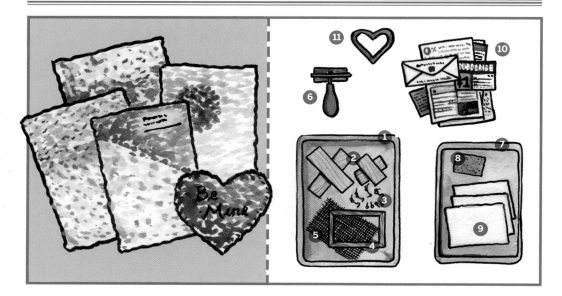

TERMS

Mold and deckle The frame that's used to make paper. The *mold* is the bottom portion, which includes the stiff mesh that the screen rests on. The *deckle* is the upper portion, which determines the shape and size of the sheet of paper (the ragged edges seen in handmade papers are called deckle edges). There are many different versions of this mold and deckle setup; for this project we use a variation called a deckle box or pour mold.

Couching Pronounced "cooching" (it's derived from the French *coucher*, "to lay"), this is the process of transferring the wet sheet from the mold to another surface (the felt) to dry.

Felts Sometimes called couching sheets, these are the pieces of material used to separate sheets of wet paper while they dry. Felts are available at art supply shops; however, interfacing or old wool army blankets can also work well.

Pulp The mix of water and plant fibers that your paper is made of. You can create pulp from cotton linters (sold at art supply stores) and other plant fibers, but in this project we'll make pulp by reusing scrap paper and junk mail.

MATERIALS

1. VAT SUCH AS A RUBBERMAID TUB OR OTHER WATERPROOF CONTAINER
2. 1"×4" LUMBER CUT TO TWO 5" PIECES AND TWO 9" PIECES
3. HOOK AND EYE LATCHES (4)
4. CANVAS STRETCHER, SOLD AT ART SUPPLY STORES
5. WINDOW SCREENING
6. BRAYER OR ANY SMOOTH, FLAT BLOCK
7. COOKIE SHEET OR OTHER SURFACE FOR WATER CONTROL
8. SPONGE
9. INTERFACING OR WOOL BLANKETS FOR FELTS
10. OLD BILLS, JUNK MAIL, AND OTHER SCRAP PAPERS, AND INCLUSIONS (OPTIONAL) SUCH AS FABRIC OR PAPER SCRAPS, GLITTER, LEAVES, OR FLOWER PETALS
11. COOKIE CUTTERS (OPTIONAL)

NOT SHOWN
» BLENDER
» HAMMER
» STAPLE GUN

START »

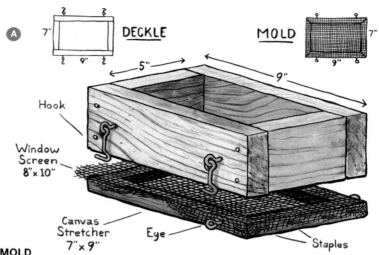

A   7"   DECKLE   MOLD   7"

9"   9"

5"   9"

Hook

Window
Screen
8" x 10"

Canvas
Stretcher
7" x 9"   Eye

Staples

1. BUILD THE POUR MOLD

1a. Cut the window screening to a size slightly larger than the outside dimensions of the canvas stretcher (my canvas stretcher here is 7"×9"). Use a staple gun to attach the window screening mesh to the canvas stretcher, making sure it's as taut as possible.

1b. Cut 4 pieces of 1"×4" lumber (here my pieces were 5" and 9" long) to fit together into a rectangle

— the interior size will be the finished size of your paper (5"×7" in this case). Secure the sides with wood glue and nails.

1c. Add the hook and eye latches on either side of the mold and deckle box to hold them together tightly.

2. MAKE THE PULP

The paper you choose to recycle will affect the consistency, color, and feel of your handmade paper. In general, bills and printer papers will create a smoother, more consistent sheet, while magazine pages and glossy papers will tend to chop up more irregularly, creating a more "artistic" look. Experiment with mixing different papers together.

2a. Cut or tear your paper into approximately 1" square pieces, and place them in the blender with enough water to cover them completely. With the pour method, you can make as much pulp as you want at a time; a good rule of thumb is that whatever the size of your original sheet, the pulp you make from it will make a sheet about 1" smaller in both width and length.

2b. Blend the paper scraps and water until all large chunks are pulverized (about 30 seconds to 1 minute). The longer you blend the pulp, the smoother and more regular your paper will be. Pulping can dull your blender's blades quickly, so it's a good idea to keep a dedicated papermaking blade or get a separate blender (you can usually find one at a thrift store) if you want to make paper frequently.

2c. Personalize your pulp! You can add in a wide variety of materials while blending, including leaves, flowers, glitter, confetti, seeds, and much more. It's best not to blend ribbons or other long fibers, as they can get wound around the blades. Finally, consider dyeing your pulp (see "101: Natural Dyeing" in CRAFT, Volume 04, page 148).

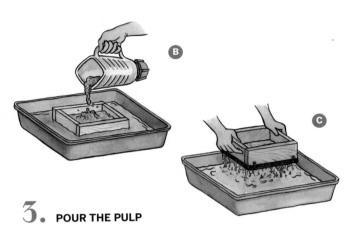

3. POUR THE PULP

3a. Fill your vat with enough water to cover the mesh on the resting pour mold by at least ½". (A large Rubbermaid tub works great, and can be used to store your papermaking supplies when not in use.)

3b. Using the hook and eye latches, secure the deckle box and the mold. Place them in the vat, sliding in at an angle to discourage air pockets from forming.

3c. Pour your pulp onto the mesh (Figure B). The more pulp poured, the thicker the paper. Use your fingers or a spoon to stir the pulp and distribute the fibers evenly across the surface of the water.

Slowly pull the pour mold upward, letting the water drain back into the tub (Figure C). Place the entire apparatus on a cookie sheet to keep water from getting everywhere.

4. COUCH THE SHEET

4a. Undo the hook and eye latches and lift the deckle box, being careful not to pull the wet sheet up with it (Figure D).

4b. Lay your felt (I used interfacing for this project) onto the wet sheet (Figure E). Carefully turn over the felt, sheet, and mold (Figure F). Be sure to hold the layers together.

4c. Use a sponge to soak up any excess water from the sheet, pressing down on top of the felt and wringing out the sponge until you can't pull any more water out of the paper (Figure G).

4d. Slowly lift the mold from the paper surface, holding down the felt (Figure H). The surface tension between the felt and the paper is greater

than that between the paper and the mesh, which should cause the paper to stick to the felt.

4e. Place another felt piece on top of the sheet. Using a brayer or presser bar (or any smooth, even surface), smooth the paper to remove any lingering excess moisture (Figure I).

5. DRY THE PAPER

Set the paper between the felts on a flat surface to air-dry. Your paper may "cockle" (curl) a bit; if you want to reduce cockling, stack your wet sheets, one on top of the other, with felts between each sheet, then place a heavy book on top to press them (Figure J).

The drying time of your papers will vary from less than an hour to several days, depending on the humidity in the air and the type of pulp used. If the drying takes more than a day, change the felts once a day — this will keep the paper from getting moldy. If you're in a hurry, you can gently press your sheets with an iron, but this tends to make the sheets cockle quite a bit, and I don't recommend it.

FINISH ⊠

VARIATIONS »

Paper Shapes

You can easily incorporate designs into your paper by separating different pulp colors or textures into simple designs.

A piece of stiff, thin plastic can split your sheet into 2 or more sections. You can also use cookie cutters or a tin can with both ends removed (for circles, as seen in the opening shot) to create shapes within your sheet, or to make shaped gift tags, etc.

Pour distinct pulp mixtures into the separated areas, pull your mold from the vat, and remove the separators before couching your sheet. The pressure

from the felt will join the separate sections into a single sheet, as long as they're approximately the same density and weight.

Embedded Items

If you'd like to embed flat items such as paper, fabric, or leaves into your paper, it's easy. Dip the item into your pulp mixture to coat it with a thin layer, and then work the item into the pulp sheet right after you remove it from the vat.

François Vigneault is a cartoonist, publisher, and occasional bird-watcher. *Friends* is his catchall personal comic book; he is also the editor of *Elfworld*. He thanks you, deeply, for your interest. family-style.com

JUMPING
PAPER FROG

Just cut, fold, and clip to make
a super cute, hopping toy.

By Matt Hawkins

Photography and illustration by Matt Hawkins

MATERIALS

» **Frog template** Download from craftzine.com/play/05.

» **Paper clips (2)** about 2" long

» **White glue**

» **Scissors or X-Acto knife**

» **Printer and printer paper**

I t's like a matter transporter. An artist creates a 3D object, and it's flattened out and sent through cyberspace as a bunch of ones and zeros, only to be reassembled as a 3D object half a world away. That's just one of the things I love about online paper toys.

Right now, there seems to be an explosion of free, online, designer paper toys. It's the rage of the age. Lots of artists and designers have free paper toys on their sites nowadays. It's the natural evolution of the whole vinyl toy phenomenon: more grassroots and DIY.

Paper breaks down a lot of the barriers that otherwise keep an artist from making a toy. It eliminates cost restrictions for both artist and fan, distribution can be anywhere in the world, and supply is unlimited. Anyone with an internet connection, a printer, and half an hour to waste can own these paper toys. But their real value is in the joy the artist gets out of designing and sharing them, and the play the builder gets out of making and displaying them. Paper to the people!

Matt Hawkins makes paper toys. He shares them with the world at custompapertoys.com. He's always drawing comics or doodling or playing the banjo or something.

Did you ever do that old grade school trick with the paper clip where you make it jump off the desk? If you did, this project will bring back memories.

1. CUT, FOLD, AND GLUE THE TEMPLATE

Clip out the paper frog template on the solid lines right out of this magazine. You can also color-copy the template first, or download it from craftzine.com/05/play if you don't want to harm your magazine or if you need a second frog for a jumping contest. A blank DIY frog template is also available online for the artistically inclined.

Most paper toys should be printed on cardstock or thick, matte photo paper, but you can print this little guy on regular paper. Be sure to cut the 2 slots in the bottom panel and around the top of the eyes. Fold on the dotted lines, then glue the tabs in numerical order to form the frog's body.

2. SHAPE THE PAPER CLIP

Take the outside end and the inside hook of the paper clip and pull them out into a triangle. Bend the clip so the long end is just barely touching the hook part at the bend (Figure A). Hold the triangle so the touching ends are away from you. Push the hook end down and pull the straight end toward you.

⚠️ **WARNING: You are soon going to have a jumping paper clip on your hands. Don't put your face above it once it's loaded.**

To cock the paper clip, place the straight end back behind the hook end. It will want to come back forward. You may need to bend the sides of the triangle out a bit so the 2 ends are just barely holding each other back. You'll want to get it so close that it pops a couple of times before it just barely hangs on.

Once the paper clip is "loaded," lightly hold the triangle between your thumb and index finger so that the long part is on top and will spring downward. Gently tap the paper clip flat on the table and — boing! — it should spring into the air. This might take a little practice if you've never done it before.

The farther you bend the ends apart, the higher the paper clip should jump. The paper clip will eventually lose its springiness, so you'd better raid the office supply closet for plenty.

3. LOAD THE FROG

After you get the hang of the jumping paper clip, take the long end of the paper clip and feed it in the first slot and out the second slot on the bottom of the frog. Feed the paper clip past the first bend in the clip so the open part of the paper clip is at the back corner of the frog. The hook part of the paper clip should rest on the frog's bottom, while the straight piece is up in the air (Figure B).

Turn the frog upside down, then cock and hold the paper clip as before, resting the frog's body on top. Gently slam your fingers on the table, and there you have the jumping paper frog (Figure C)!

Resources for fantastic and free paper toys:

Custom Paper Toys (my site): custompapertoys.com
NiceBunny: nicebunny.com/new/toys.html
Readymech: readymech.fwis.com
Speakerdog: bentheillustrator.com/speakerdog_index.html
Toypaper: toypaper.co.uk
Paper Forest: paperforest.blogspot.com

Craft Holiday Gift Guide

There's no need to leave your house to shop this holiday season as there's a growing online crafty wonderland filled with handmade goods perfect for everyone on your gift list. Here are a few favorites:

Buy Olympia
buyolympia.com
Everything handmade from guitar straps to soap to stickers to kids' books.

Indie Fixx
indiefixx.com
Check out the extensive holiday gift guide and daily finds.

Cut + Paste
cutxpaste.com
Shop for crafts, paper goods, clothing, accessories, and zines.

Mahar Dry Goods
mahardrygoods.com
Stylishly cute baby and kid stuff.

Etsy
etsy.com
Handmade wares by more than 3,000 sellers, featuring anything under the sun.

Modish
modish.typepad.com
A blog and shop featuring indie jewelry, homewares, and more.

Fred Flare
fredflare.com
Fashionably kitschy finds and lots of great gifts under $25.

Rare Bird Finds
rarebirdfinds.typepad.com
Shopping blog with great indie finds for the home.

❄ Don't miss our complete CRAFT holiday gift guide this holiday season on craftzine.com.

BAZAAR

CRAFTY GOODS WE ADORE. *Compiled by Natalie Zee Drieu*

Fruit Head Gang Dolls

$60
sewingstars.com

Sewing Stars' Teresa Levy brings fruit to life with her Fruit Head Gang of stuffed collector's dolls. My favorite is the Granny Smith Apple Head Girl who's in need of some cheering up! Each doll seems to have its own personality, and Levy's detailed handiwork is apparent, from stitched leaves to stylish dresses. Also check out the rest of the gang and friends: Red Delicious Apple Head Girl, Strawberry Head Girl, and the Ice Cream Dolls.

Shannon Okey Hand-dyed Yarn for Stitch Cleveland
$30-40
stitchcleveland.com

Knitgrrl Shannon Okey's merino wool hand-dyed, washable yarns come in a variety of colors named after her friends (famous knitters and crocheters, no doubt) as well as other things she likes. I love the variety of rich colors and tones that are perfect for any of your fiber projects. Pictured here, clockwise from top left: Glampyre, Eleanor, Yarn Harlot, and Rainbow.

Stitchable Paper Journal Kits
$22
amhdesignonline.com

Bringing her love of needlepoint to paper, Amy Holbrook helps you make your journal feel like a personal heirloom with her stitchable journal kits. Choose from three brightly patterned journal designs filled with 192 unlined pages. Each journal has a special laser-etched cover with holes so you can needlepoint your initials in less than an hour. The kit comes with a full set of instructions, threads, needles, and a chart of all letters for the initials.

Bella Blue Hand-painted Knitting Needles and Crochet Hooks
$38 needles, $26 hooks
bellablue.net

I'm a fan of these leopard-print knitting needles — while I love the simple lines of my regular bamboo pairs, there's something about these that makes me smile. They're just the thing to cheer you up about a particularly tricky stretch of knitting!

Beth Bess, the designer, spent a year working on the finish so that the yarn doesn't snag, and they are as smooth as can be. Over time, the paint wears ever so slightly, but that just adds to their charm. New patterns are in the works.

—Arwen O'Reilly

Selvedge Magazine

$90/year
selvedge.org

It's impossible to describe *Selvedge* without sounding like a babbling idiot. With everything from histories of linen or tweed or subway car upholstery to the politics of Dutch wax resist fabrics to profiles of contemporary designers, you immediately sense what they call a "cerebral and sensual addiction to textiles in all forms." Turn the way you think about fabric upside down, whether it's woven, painted, knit, or felted, art, fashion, or craft. —*AO'R*

 ## Hambly Screen Prints

Overlays $3 per sheet, rub-on transfers $5
hamblyscreenprints.com

Now you can paper-craft with an edge, with funky overlays and rub-on transfers by Hambly Screen Prints. All products are hand-silk-screened with rich metallic, transparent, and opaque inks to give your projects the necessary dosage of cool grittiness or modern elegance. Choose from a variety of designs, from skulls, DJ turntables, and birds, to vintage borders and chandeliers. The transparent overlays and rub-on transfers will help take your personalized cards, gift tags, photo albums, or scrapbooks to another crafty level.

Cathy of California Mushroom Pincushion

$32
cathyofcalifornia.etsy.com

My sewing corner isn't complete without my green mushroom pincushion by Cathy of California. I love the vintage look of the 60s, and this burlap-covered pincushion with kitschy ribbon straw flowers is the perfect décor piece that makes me happy each time I look at it. It comes in a variety of vibrant colors, and with the large styrofoam mushroom head, you'll always have plenty of room for all your pins!

7oz Upholsterer's Tack Hammer

$20
hammersource.com

I recently took an upholstery class and fell head-over-heels for my teacher's magnetic tack hammer. Light and elegant, one end of the hammer is magnetized to pick up super-sharp upholstery tacks so you can stretch fabric with one hand and tap a tack in with the other. Flip the hammer around to the heavier face and finish the job. I immediately bought one for myself, and now spend my days dreaming up new projects to use it for. What doesn't need to be tacked down, really?

—*AO'R*

CRAFT LOOKS AT BOOKS

» Crochet Me: Designs to Fuel the Crochet Revolution

By Kim Werker Interweave Press, $22
crochetmebook.com

I can't seem to get enough of crochet this year! Giving the crochet world a high-kick is Kim Werker with her new book, *Crochet Me*. This book reinvigorates the craft to new fashion heights. Cuddle up in Robyn Chachula's Comfy Cardi or hit the town in Amy O'Neill Houck's Babydoll Dress. Join in on more fun online with the Crochet Me Crochet Along (crochetmealong.blogspot.com).

» KnitKnit: Profiles + Projects from Knitting's New Wave

By Sabrina Gschwandtner Stewart, Tabori & Chang, $30
stcbooks.com

I've been reading *KnitKnit* magazine for years now, and the book is everything it promised and more. It's the first knitting book that takes knitting really seriously, with a fantastic breadth of profiles and patterns ranging from artists to knitwear designers to activists. *KnitKnit* gets across that knitting has power as a social force and a political one, but no one represented here forgets that most importantly of all, knitting is beautiful. —*AO'R*

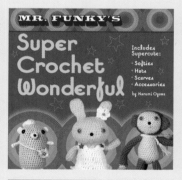

» Mr. Funky's Super Crochet Wonderful

By Narumi Ogawa North Light Books, $13
misterfunky.com

Last May at Maker Faire my daughter bought the most adorable brown crochet elephant. I immediately recognized it as one of Narumi Ogawa's hip Japanese-inspired creations. Now she's come out with a book that shows us how we can make our own "crochet wonderfuls." From amigurumi bunnies and cuddly snakes to motif scarves, funky hats, and flower earrings, this book is for anyone with a weak spot for the super-cute. —*Carla Sinclair*

» Softies: Simple Instructions for 25 Plush Pals

By Therese Laskey Chronicle Books, $20
chroniclebooks.com

I've been addicted to Therese Laskey's Softies Central blog (softies central.typepad.com) for a long time now. In her new book, *Softies*, she's rounded up a wide variety of plush toys and goodies from an international list of crafters we all know and love. Sew up one of Heidi Kenney's adorable felt ice cream sandwiches or Cassi Griffin's sweet flowery pincushions. Most of these projects help you use up your craft stash, and the ready-to-use pattern sheets are a lifesaver!

DEAR TUCKER,
I'VE BEEN MEANING TO WRITE YOU THIS LETTER FOR SOME TIME. NOW IN MY TRAVELS, I THINK I SHOULD SAY HOW I FEEL.

I WOULD HAVE SENT THIS TO YOU VIA EMAIL, BUT IT'S IMPOSSIBLE TO FIND A CONNECTION THIS DEEP IN THE HIMALAYAS.

LUCKILY THE LOCAL MONKS SHARED SOME OF THEIR ANCIENT MEANS OF COMMUNICATION WITH ME.

FIRST, THEY SHOWED ME HOW TO MAKE INK!

PEN

DID YOU KNOW? BY SQUASHING BERRIES, EVEN FROZEN ONES, YOU CAN MAKE INK. A 1/2 CUP O FRESH BERRIES IS PLEN PUSH THEM THROUGH A STRAINER, GETTING THE BERRY JUICE PULP-FREE.

ALONG WITH THE BERRY JUICE, 2 KEY INGREDIENTS ARE SALT AND VINEGAR. 1/2 TEASPOON OF VINEGAR WILL HELP TO HOLD THE COLOR. 1/2 TEASPOON OF SALT ACTS AS A NICE PRESERVATIVE.

WHAT'S INK WITHOUT PAPER? I NEVER KNEW THAT MONKS ARE SO SELF-SUFFICIENT.

THEY RECYCLE ALL OF THEIR PAPER. WHEN THEY SHOWED ME HOW TO MAKE IT, I WAS ENCOURAGED TO EXPERIMENT WITH MIXING DIFFERENT TYPES OF PAPER.

FIRST, YOU'LL NEED A BLENDER. FILL IT UP HALF WAY WITH PAPER AND THE FILL THE REST WITH WAR WATER. BLEND UNTIL NO PAPER FLAKES REMAIN.

ONCE YOU HAVE SMOOTH PULP, YOU WILL NEED A MOLD. NOTHING WORKS BETTER THAN A PIECE OF SCREEN FROM A WINDOW AND AN OLD PICTURE FRAME. STAPLE TOGETHER AND VOILÀ!

FILL A SMALL TUB WITH THE BLENDED PULP. STIR IN 2 TEASPOONS OF LIQUID STARCH — IT'LL HELP PREVENT THE BERRY INK FROM BLEEDING.

SUBMERGE THE MOLD INTO THE PULP. GENTLY WIGGLE IT, UNTIL THE PULP'S THICK ENOUGH AND EVENLY LAID ON THE SCREEN.

TUB

FABRIC

LIFT THE MOLD OUT OF THE WATER TO DRAIN. THIS IS A GOOD TIME TO JUDGE THE THICKNESS OF YOUR PAPER. MORE PULP WILL THICKEN THE PAPER, LESS WILL MAKE IT THINNER.

CAREFULLY LOWER THE MOLD, PULP SIDE DOWN, ONTO A PIECE OF FABRIC.

USE A SPONGE TO PRESS AND SOAK UP EXCESS WATER.

WHILE THE PULP IS STILL WET, SLOWLY LIFT THE MOLD, SEPARATING IT FROM THE PAPER PULP. THIS MAY TAKE A FEW TRIES. THE KEY IS TO KEEP THE PAPER FROM TEARING.

USE A TOP LAYER OF FABRIC ON THE PAPER TO PRESS OUT AND FLATTEN THE SHEET.

HANG UP TO DRY!

I'VE SEEN THE MONKS CREATE MANY BEAUTIFUL AND TEXTURED PAPERS. MIXING DIFFERENT MATERIALS SUCH AS SMALL TWIGS, SCRAPS OF FOIL, AND EVEN FLOWERS, YOU CAN ADD ALL KINDS OF FLAVORS TO YOUR PAPERS.

LASTLY, THE MONKS TAUGHT ME HOW TO MAKE A QUILL USING A FEATHER. LARGER FEATHERS WORK BEST.

BY SOAKING THE STEM IN HOT WATER AND USING A PAIR OF TWEEZERS, YOU'LL REMOVE THE MEMBRANE FROM THE INSIDE OF THE STEM.

NEXT, YOU'LL NEED TO THOROUGHLY DRY THE STEM. SIT IT IN A DRY PLACE. STICKING IT IN HOT SAND WORKS BEST.

HOT   HOT

PAL

CUTTING THE STEM IS MOST IMPORTANT FOR CLEAN LINES. CHECK OUT MY DRAWINGS TO SEE HOW THE TIP NEEDS TO BE CARVED.

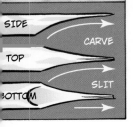

SIDE

CARVE

TOP

SLIT

BOTTOM

TOGETHER WITH QUILL, PAPER, AND INK, I'M READY TO CREATE! I'VE BEEN KEEPING A JOURNAL (THAT I MADE) DURING MY JOURNEY. I LOVE TO SIT AND RECORD ALL OF MY THOUGHTS. I EVEN HAVE A SECTION OF DRAWINGS OF ALL THE WONDERFUL SIGHTS I'VE SEEN! ANYWAY ...

THE REAL POINT OF THIS LETTER WAS TO TELL YOU HOW MUCH I MISS YOU. BEING SO FAR AWAY HAS MADE ME REALIZE THAT I REALLY VALUE YOUR FRIENDSHIP. YOU SHARE MY CURIOSITY FOR THE WORLD, AND ARE ALWAYS URGING ME ON TO EVER CRAZIER ADVENTURES. PLUS YOU ALWAYS KEEP ME SMILING. YOU'RE MY BEST FRIEND, TUCK! WISH YOU WERE HERE,

CELINE

END

Susan Beal
Recycle It

» Susan Beal is a writer and designer. She co-wrote *Super Crafty: Over 75 Amazing How-to Projects*, and her jewelry, skirt kits, and writing can be found at susanstars.com and westcoastcrafty.com.

Vintage Sheet Revival

Reincarnate a sheet into a belt, a sunglasses case, and an apron.

Upcycling a vintage sheet gives you yards and yards of cool fabric to work with, so the sky's the limit when it comes to project ideas. I made this little matching set — a belt, sunglasses case, and craft apron — with a flowered sheet I spotted at a yard sale for $1. I even had enough left over to make 4 more of everything!

Since vintage sheet fabric is so soft to the touch, I added topstitching all around the edges of each piece to keep the lines crisp, and lined each project with batting, interfacing, or a second layer of material.

These pieces are all quick to make and beginner-friendly. Add your own touches to make them super personalized, too!

SUNGLASSES CASE

This case is designed for a pair of vintage sunglasses with round, oversized frames. You may want to streamline it a bit if yours are sleeker!

1. Cut 2 pieces of fabric and 1 piece of batting, each 7"×8". Stack them right sides together, with the batting underneath, and use pins to mark the halfway point across the top, and 2" down on the right side, as shown (Figure A).

2. Use a rotary cutter or sharp scissors to cut a diagonal line between the 2 points you marked. Now flip the stack over so that the batting is on top, and trim it ¼" smaller than the fabric on all sides. Pin the stack together on both sides and the top (Figure B).

3. Using a medium-length straight stitch, sew all around the 3 pinned sides, following the edge of the batting, and leaving the bottom section open.

Materials

- » **Vintage sheet**
- » **Sewing machine**
- » **Sharp scissors**
- » **Measuring tape**
- » **Rotary cutter (recommended)**
- » **Quilt ruler (recommended)**
- » **Cutting mat (recommended)**
- » **Straight pins**
- » **Iron**
- » **Ironing board**

For the sunglasses case:
- » **A small piece of quilt batting**

For the belt:
- » **¼ yard of interfacing**
- » **1½" D-rings (2)**

Photography by Susan Beal

4. Clip all the corners and turn it right side out so the batting is tucked inside. Iron the entire piece, then fold the lower raw edges over ¼" and press them to the inside, so they're hidden within the layers. Pin them in place. Now topstitch all along the upper edge, leaving the sides unstitched (Figure C).

5. Fold the case vertically along the centerline so that the sides meet, and pin them together. Re-pin the bottom so it's folded flat and secured with a single layer of pins. Now topstitch from the upper right corner all the way down and around to the mid-left side, so the case is sealed on 3 sides. Slip your favorite sunglasses inside (Figure D)!

BELT

The measurements given make a belt that's 42" long. Just add or subtract length from the 44" raw measurement to change the size.

1. Cut a 44"×3" piece of fabric and a 43"×2¼" piece of interfacing. You may need to overlap 2 shorter pieces of interfacing if yours is shorter than 43".

2. Use a hot iron to fuse the interfacing to the wrong side of the fabric, following label instructions and centering it on the material (Figure E).

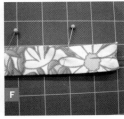

3. Clip all 4 corners and fold and press both ends of the fabric over ½" to the interfacing/wrong side of the fabric. Now begin folding and pressing the long edges of the fabric the same way, so it's neatly folded over the interfacing layer, and pin it every few inches. Press both sides the same way.

4. Fold and press the belt together down the center, the long way, securing the open edges with pins (Figure F).

5. Starting at one end, begin topstitching along the open side, sewing near the edge with a medium-length straight stitch. Topstitch both ends and the folded side so that the entire belt is neatly edged with stitching.

6. Slip the 2 D-rings onto one end of the belt and mark 1½" from the end. Bring the end to that spot and stitch it in place, catching both of the D-rings in the loop so they move freely (Figure G). That's it!

CRAFT APRON

This apron uses a double layer of material so it's durable, and the deep pockets will hold lots of your craft supplies while you work.

1. Cut one 68"×3" piece of material for the apron tie and a 44"×22" piece for the body (Figure H).

2. Fold the larger piece in half, right sides together, so that you have a 22" square. Pin and stitch both sides, leaving the top open, and clip the bottom corners. Turn it right side out and use a chopstick or pencil to fold the corners out to neat points. Topstitch all along the bottom edge.

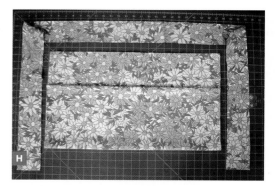

3. Mark 8" from the bottom and fold there, bringing the bottom edge toward the top, and creating your pocket layer (Figure I). Pin both sides. Topstitch both sides, catching the folded section, and continuing to the top of the apron body.

4. Decide how wide you want your pockets to be — you can make 2 identical ones, 4 of varying widths, or anything in between. I chose to make mine with 3 equal-sized pockets. Mark where you want to define the pockets, and stitch those places from the top of the fold downward to secure them (Figure J).

5. Now create your apron ties. Like Steps 3 and 4 in the belt instructions, press the raw edges inside and fold the whole thing the long way, but don't use interfacing. Pin all around the open edge of the ties (Figure J).

6. Mark the center 23" of the opening in the tie and leave it open; this section becomes the waistband. Topstitch all around the rest of the waistband, including the top edge and both sides.

7. Now tuck the upper edge of the apron body into the waistband, pinning it into place. Stitch this final seam, matching the topstitching at both sides (Figure K). You're done!

» EMBELLISHMENT IDEAS:
I added vintage buttons as flower centers on my sunglasses case and cut a simple petal shape out of wool felt to decorate my apron pocket, stitching it on with another favorite button. Try adding lace, ribbon, trim, or appliqués to customize yours! ✂

Wine Sleeve

Heading to a dinner party with a bottle of wine? Paper and plastic bags are so 1990s. Take an old long-sleeved shirt to create this reusable wine sleeve. You can use a favorite vintage shirt to hold a favorite vintage wine, if you don't mind losing the sleeves. (For extra credit, wear the shirt when you present the wine.)

You will need: A long-sleeved shirt with a hem at the wrist, 2 cords for a drawstring, needle and thread or sewing machine, fabric scissors, safety pin

1. Choose a shirt.

Select a long-sleeved shirt with a hem around the wrist. The hem will become the casing for the drawstring.

2. Cut the sleeve.

Cut off the sleeve near the armpit. Most wine bottles are about 1 foot tall, so make sure you have a few extra inches.

3. Flip and sew.

Turn the sleeve inside out and stitch along the unhemmed edge, sewing the edge shut. Then flip the sleeve back to the right side.

4. Cut slits for the drawstring.

Take your scissors and cut 2 small slits in the hem directly across from each other.

5. Create the drawstring.

Take one of your cords and attach a safety pin to the end. Thread the cord though the hemmed edge of the sleeve, beginning and ending at the same point. Remove the safety pin and double knot the ends together. Repeat with the second cord on the opposite side. Once you've secured the second cord with a double knot, pull the drawstrings away from each other, and you've created your wine pouch. Add your favorite bottle and enjoy.

Variation:

Cut the sleeve from a short-sleeved shirt to make a mini-pouch for holding a camera, art supplies, MP3 player, or other small objects.

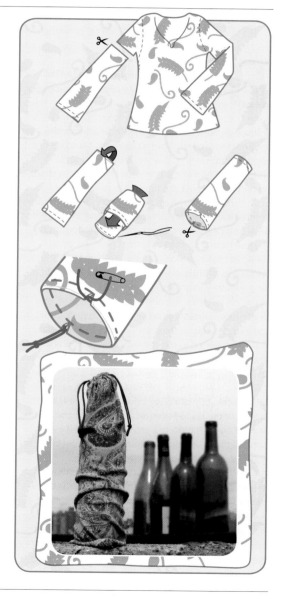

Illustration by Tim Lillis; photograph by Tiffany Threadgould

Tiffany Threadgould is a design junkie and the author of the *This into That* books. Her business, RePlayGround (replayground.com), sells recycled goods, features DIY projects, and accepts donations of your unwanted items.

Wendy Tremayne
Re: Fitted

» Wendy Tremayne (gaiatreehouse.com) is renovating an RV park into a 100% reuse off-grid B&B in Truth or Consequences, N.M. Another project, Swap-O-Rama-Rama (swaporamarama.org), is a clothing swap and DIY workshop designed to offer people an alternative to consumerism.

Over-the-Shoulder Holder: Bra Conversion

Between 50 and 100 bras clutter Itsi Atkins' New York City apartment. Ranging in size from 32A to 50I, many of them have been transformed from underwear to outerwear and now await contents to fill their cups and a shoulder to carry them away. These bras have become handbags, backpacks, and water bottle holders.

The leap from undergarment to purse is not arbitrary. The bra and the handbag, Atkins explains, have three common and necessary design characteristics: structure, shape, and style. Both items have one primary purpose: to hold. Accordingly, "A perfect bra creates a perfect bag," he says.

Atkins' "flash fashion" can be found on the famous shoulders of Hollywood stars such as Carol Channing, Helen Mirren, and Leelee Sobieski, to name a few. He relishes the cleverness of the pun, and describes his designs as a coming together of social and political statements merged with popular culture, typified in his recent Paris Hilton ankle bracelet purse. The handbag, he explains, "is like a small moving billboard as it is carried around town."

Once a maker views the bra as a creative material, a world of possibility opens. Bras can be found in seemingly endless patterns, textures, and colors. Adorned with thematic accoutrements, they satisfy people of all sizes and temperaments. The various types of bras offer built-in design possibilities. Under-wire bras make great water bottle holders, while very large bras transform into useful backpacks, and silky bras convert to fancy evening bags.

Atkins invites us to look at the bra with new eyes. He sees a garment whose structure, design, and ornamentation is like no other. And he points out that the bra's utilitarian applications have hardly been explored. With a snicker, Atkins invites the maker to take to the street an article of clothing that at one time might have held the image of their libido.

Two of Itsi Atkins' bras gone bag.

Photography by Itsi Atkins

MATERIALS NEEDED FOR BOTH PROJECTS:
Underwire bra, scissors, needle and thread or glue

BASIC BRA-TO-HANDBAG CONVERSION

1. Cut bra into 3 parts: straps, backside, and cup side. When cutting, leave a 1" seam allowance of extra fabric from the backside to the right and left of the cups. The remaining backside will be discarded.

2. Fold the cups over so the interiors face one another. Turn the project upside down on your work surface.

3. Stitch or glue the 2 cups together along the sides and bottom, leaving the top open so that it becomes the handbag's opening.

4. Add the straps by sewing them along what was the bottom of the bra. A zipper or button can be added as a means of closing the top.

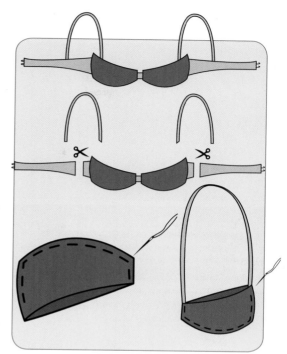

OVER-THE-SHOULDER WATER BOTTLE HOLDER

1. Cut the shoulder straps where they attach to the back of the bra. Leave them attached to the front of the bra. Tie or sew the ends of these straps together. This will become your water bottle strap.

2. Cut a hole the size of a quarter in the center of one cup of the bra. The cap of your water bottle will fit through this opening. Cut a second hole to the side of the cup, next to the underwire, above the first hole. This hole will allow one portion of the back of the bra to be pulled through the other. Finally, cut a third hole that will accommodate the water bottle's cap, halfway down the other back strap.

3. Place the water bottle's cap through the first hole (the hole in the center of the cup) and pull the bra down over the bottle on both sides.

4. Place the base of the water bottle in the uncut bra cup. Wrap the 2 sides of the bra around the bottle's bottom and back up again, now on opposite sides. When the longer side of the bra meets the second hole, insert it into the hole and pull it through. Wrap until the third hole meets and fits over the water bottle cap. Now connect the bra hook and eyes and decorate to your liking. ✄

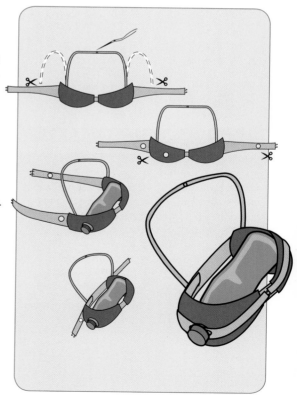

Etsy

Etsy.com
Your place to buy and sell all things handmade.

Jewelry
RaesCreations $33

Toys
tinywarbler $25

Bath & Beauty
naiad $5

Clothing
asianicandy $65

Children
maximummouse $24

Art
joncarling $7

Woodworking
segmental $200

Housewares
Whamodyne $15

Housewares
Bombus $240

Books & Zines
ArtisanGraham $130

Supplies
petitespoon $7

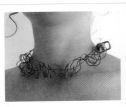

Jewelry
bronwenhandcrafted $65

Bags & Purses
DrikaB $55

Accessories
QuietDoing $19

Clothing
desirapesta $135

Ceramics & Pottery
foldedpigs $12

Jewelry
honeybee $245

Paper Goods
annacote $10

Housewares
joom $28

Children
jasperheartswren $35

Accessories
bossybootsdesign $50

Glass
SolosGlass $149.99

Plants & Edibles
VeganHoney $12

Music
goodfeets $200

Housewares
girlscantell $9.75

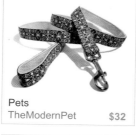

Pets
TheModernPet $32

Furniture
modernfront $1215

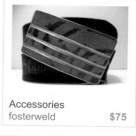

Accessories
fosterweld $75

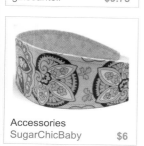

Accessories
SugarChicBaby $6

Candles
StudioNoirCandles $7.50

Clothing
Tenlittlefingers $90

Art
yellena $20

Bags & Purses
hollyhawk $48

Toys
usnavyretiredvet $13.95

Housewares
LightingArtGallery $275

Housewares
PataPri $14

The items above were selected from the over **650,000 handmade goods** for sale on Etsy. Find any of the items above for sale, each in their own shops. Go to: shopname.etsy.com

Buy Handmade

Etsy is proud to be a supporting partner of The Handmade Pledge. Take the pledge yourself at http://www.buyhandmade.org.

Pimp My Bookcart

Last year, the online comic strip *Unshelved*, which is set in a library, ran a contest called Pimp My Bookcart. When Katie George got wind of the competition, she rounded up a dozen teen volunteers to help her brainstorm for ideas. "They came up with so many good ones!" says George, coordinator of teen programs at Howard County Library in Columbia, Md. After considering a Batmobile, a train, and a fire engine with a working siren, they decided to create a pink Cadillac, which "seemed to embody the quintessential 'pimped' ride."

When selecting materials, "we had to choose those that were nontoxic, cost-effective, and easy to work with in the library," says George. So they carved horns and fins out of styrofoam, upholstered the "seats" with white vinyl, attached working, battery-operated headlights, and covered it all in latex paint. The project took 24 hours over eight weeks.

"For most teens, working with their hands is an unusual experience," George says. "They can most often be found sitting in front of the computer." But their creativity paid off — *Pink Cadillac* won first place and now lives in the teen section of their library, holding an ongoing book display.   —*Carla Sinclair*

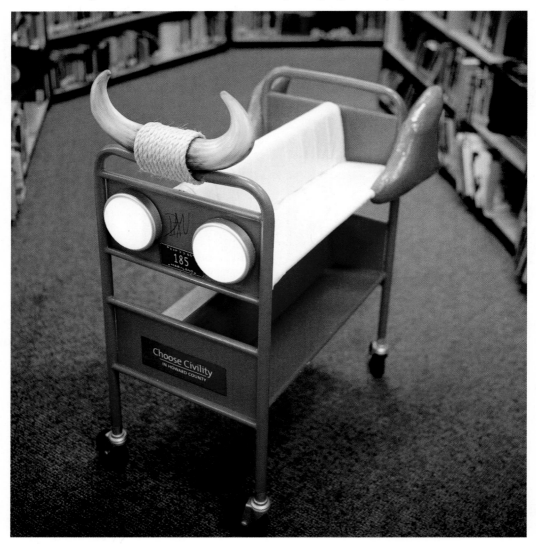

Photograph by Erika Larsen